TEACHING PHYSICS:
a guide for the non-specialist

J. OSBORNE
Lecturer in Science Education, King's (KQC) College, London
J. FREEMAN
Science Adviser, Birmingham Education Authority

CAMBRIDGE
UNIVERSITY PRESS

PUBLISHED BY THE PRESS SYNDICATE OF THE UNIVERSITY OF CAMBRIDGE
The Pitt Building, Trumpington Street, Cambridge CB2 1RP, United Kingdom

CAMBRIDGE UNIVERSITY PRESS
The Edinburgh Building, Cambridge CB2 2RU, United Kingdom
40 West 20th Street, New York, NY 10011-4211, USA
10 Stamford Road, Oakleigh, Melbourne 3166, Australia

First published 1989
Reprinted 1998

Printed in the United Kingdom at the University Press, Cambridge

A catalogue record for this book is available from the British Library

ISBN 0 521 34995 8 paperback

The publishers would like to thank the following for permission to reproduce diagrams:
Figure on p6 reproduced with the permission of SCDC Publications from *Girl-friendly Science:
Avoiding Sex Bias in the Curriculum* by Barbara Smail, Longman for SCDC Publications, York
1985.
Fig. 3.7 from p31 of *Investigating Electricity* by P Warren (1983), John Murray, London.
Figs 4.1, 4.3 and 4.4. These diagrams are based on figures 2.10–2.13 in *Children's Ideas in
Science* by Driver, Guesne, Tiberghien (eds) Open University Press 1985.
Figs 7.6 permission from National Radiological Protection Board, based on Fig 4 from *Living
with Radiation* (1981).
Figs 13.1 permission from the Institute of Physics, based on Fig 1 of *Statistics Relating to Education in
Physics*.

Illustrations by Oxford Illustrators

Contents

Preface

If you are a non-physicist and are faced with the prospect of teaching physics, whether as a subject on its own, or within some form of integrated science, you may well be feeling a little overwhelmed.

Don't panic!![1]

This book is a guide to the teaching of physics. It will show how existing science teaching skills can be effectively deployed to tackle such things as the intricacies of series and parallel circuits, and how to startle your students, and not yourself, with a Van de Graaff machine.

There are two ways of using this book: you can read it all the way through or you can use it as a dip-in resource to use while planning programmes of work and individual lessons.

A book of this length cannot hope and does not intend to deal with all the physics that you might ever need, so a selection of useful textbooks is listed in appendix 2. If you don't feel secure in your grasp of some idea that we describe, it would be helpful to have one of these textbooks alongside you.

Research[2] has shown that many teachers report the prospect of teaching physics more difficult and worrying than the actuality. This book is designed to provide assistance with common problems perceived by newcomers to the teaching of physics. It aims to provide some insight into strategies for explaining difficult topics and the likely problems and misconceptions that arise from pupils.

Finally, we are not sufficiently arrogant to propose this book as *the solution* to the teaching of physics. There is a well-organised support structure for most teachers, including heads of department, science advisers and advisory teachers, the Association for Science Education, and local Teachers' Centres to whom teachers should turn for help and assistance.

Acknowledgements

We would like to thank Dr John Harris for his many helpful comments on the original draft of this book; in addition, the Max Planck Society for many hours of fruitful discussion which have contributed to the ideas in this book.

---

1 With apologies to Douglas Adams.
2 Millar R. (1987) Teaching physics as a non-specialist – A survey of the views of teachers without formal physics qualifications. Department of Education, University of York.

1

Introduction

Difficult concepts in physics

Why is physics so difficult? The mere mention that you earn your living from teaching the subject is sufficient to lead to rapid changes in conversation. Generally, people do not wish to explore a topic which has unhappy associations. Anybody picking up this book may be haunted by similar vague feelings of uncertainty about some of the ideas they are attempting to teach. Part of the answer lies in the fact that physics deals in abstractions. These ideas and laws represent our understanding of physical reality. However, other subjects such as mathematics are even more abstract. At least in physics there is the advantage of being able to illustrate arguments and ideas by demonstration or experimentation with real and concrete examples. It would be foolish to pretend that the answers are simple or evident. This book attempts to provide an insight into some of the problems of teaching physics and to provide some tentative solutions to communicating the subject.

The mature physicist has evolved a framework of associative ideas by which he or she simplifies the subject to a relatively few fundamental ideas. It is the process of assimilation and simplification that is so difficult for many. Partly this is due to the fact that we have all been scientists from a young age and, as such, we have constructed models of reality that help us to solve problems and survive. Much physics teaching attempts to tell the pupil that their firmly held ideas are erroneous, and not surprisingly, these intuitive notions are extremely tenacious. For example, in a recent A-level physics exam, candidates were asked to give possible explanations as to why a 2p coin might take 7.6 s to fall down a well, while a 1p coin took 7.5 s. Despite the fact that all pupils are taught from the age of 14 that the gravitational acceleration of all objects is the same, a substantial number of candidates commented that 'This was surprising as the heavier coin should fall faster'.

Does this evidence point to some major failing of modern physics teaching? Probably not, since this notion which was enshrined by Aristotle, survived 1600 years till the time of Galileo who demonstrated, in the infamous experiment in 1590, that this was fallacious for objects with negligible air resistance. Such ideas are remarkably tenacious because a superficial observation supports the evidence that heavier things do fall faster. Despite the ease with which Galileo's experiment can be repeated in the laboratory, the majority of pupil's everyday experience reinforces Aristotelian ideas.

A substantial body of research work has now established that pupils develop their own intuitive understanding of the physical phenomena which they experience from an early age.[1] These understandings are referred to by a

3

variety of terms in the research literature as 'misconceptions', 'alternative conceptions', 'alternative frameworks' and 'children's science'. In addition, work done by the Assessment of Performance Unit (APU) has begun to show that we are not very effective at teaching science.[2] Solomon[3,4] has shown that another reason is that the meaning that we attach to works in physics is not by any means the same as the meaning commonly attached to such words in everyday life. A typical example would be the statement by a pupil that

> 'I've got bags of energy'

Here the child views the possession of energy in egocentric terms. Energy is seen as something which is associated with animals and humans. Pupils find it hard to imagine how energy could be stored. The physicist's understanding of the word is that 'Energy is transferred when work is done' which holds a quite different meaning. Energy for the physicist is a wholly abstract quantity which is a measure of the capacity of a body to do work. It is not a fluid and has no concrete form. Another example of a clash of concepts is

> Pupil: 'We pay for the electricity we use.'

The pupil clearly sees electricity as a finite material available from sockets for which somebody must be reimbursed. Again there is some basis for this in experience when most appliances are seen as having only one wire coming from the plug. However in a formal introduction to electricity, a teacher of physics will seek to establish quantitatively, with ammeters, that the current entering a device is the same as that leaving it. Electricity is not something which is 'used up'. Electric charge is a means of transferring energy. All the electric charge which flows out of one terminal of a battery returns to the other. In the a.c. mains supply the electric charges merely oscillate about a fixed point and the average flow of charge is zero. What does get 'used' in the sense implied by the word is the available electrical energy.

Claxton (1985)[5] has made the important point that pupils are quite capable of distinguishing science into three areas: 'gut science' which is the intuitive science used to estimate whether it is feasible to cross the road or not, 'lay science' which is the science gained from the media, comics and popular journalism and 'school science'. He argues that pupils seem to be quite capable of operating with three distinct conceptual realms between which they do not perceive a conflict. This does not make the life of the physics teacher any easier.

The purpose of this book is to outline some of the main difficulties likely to be experienced in the teaching of elementary physics and to suggest ways of approaching them. It is not the purpose of a book of this length to teach physics itself. A suitable list of books that will assist here is provided in appendix 2. We have chosen in this book to concentrate on the *concepts of physics* and the means by which we think they may be taught and learnt effectively. For non-physicists, who may be teaching physics for the first time as part of an integrated science course, these are often seen as the major area of difficulty. In a recent survey[6] of non-physicists teaching physics, two features of interest emerge. First, almost invariably fewer teachers reported difficulty when teaching a topic compared to the difficulty they anticipated beforehand. Secondly, the topics which gave the most difficulty were those that may have seemed simple because they are so fundamental, while topics that are more complex are in practice simpler to teach. For instance, voltage is the idea that most teachers reported difficulty in teaching while electronics which was predicted to be difficult turned out not to present too many problems.

A notable feature missing from this book is any emphasis on the 'processes' of physics, for example observing and hypothesising. These are important and it is impossible to teach content without process or vice versa[7]. It is perhaps ironic that in a decade when there is still considerable debate between different interpretations of the method of science, depending upon whether you agree with one philosopher or science or another[8], that the science teaching community seems to have decided that there is such a clearly defined thing as scientific method which can be clearly assimilated into the syllabus. What is perhaps a better statement is that scientists do engage in certain activities such as hypothesising, observing, classifying and testing, and that children in the laboratory should be provided with an opportunity to experience these activities if they are to gain a 'feel' for 'being a scientist'.

A style of teaching that relies heavily on demonstration and exposition does not encourage this. At its worst it presents physics as a well-defined body of knowledge with no potential for the new or unusual, ultimately giving the impression that 'physics is boring'. Unfortunately new teachers of the subject may be tempted to rely on this method since it provides a secure framework within which to explore the teaching of new content. However it is notable that experienced teachers of physics use a range of classroom activities consisting of practicals, demonstrations, home experiments, group discussions, games, computer software, videos and films to provide a range of different experiences and activities for children. Less-experienced teachers should be prepared to experiment with their methods a little to avoid a rather lifeless presentation and lots of suggestions are included in this book.

In future, physics will increasingly be taught as part of modular, integrated or coordinated science courses to meet the requirement for broad and balanced science courses. One of the effects of this is the need to give serious consideration to the methods of linking the separate subject disciplines. One such scheme devised by Barbara Smail[9] for lower school science courses which is based on the human body is shown in the figure.

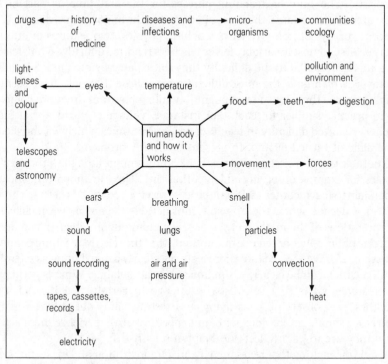

Lower School science curriculum based on the human body

The advantage of this scheme is that the interest of girls and boys in the human body and their own selves provides a motivating context for teaching and learning. Such ideas deserve serious consideration, but ultimately the teaching of physics requires good, clear, lively and enthusiastic exposition using a variety of learning strategies. We hope that this book will provide some assistance to those searching for ideas.

Notes and references

1 Readers are referred to the following books and articles which are a good overview of this research.
Driver R., Guesne E. & Tiberghien A. (eds.) (1985) *Children's Ideas in Science.* Open University Press, Milton Keynes.
Osborne R. & Freyberg P. (1985) *Learning in Science.* Heinemann, London.
Gilbert J.K. & Watts D.M. (1983) 'Concepts, misconceptions and alternative conceptions: Changing perspectives in science education.' *Studies in Science Education,* 10, 61–98.
2 The Assessment of Performance Unit (APU) has published four brief summary reports which give a detailed insight into the state of science education. These are
○ *Science at Age 11*   1984
○ *Science at Age 13*   1984

○*Science at Age 15*   1985
○*Electricity at Age 15* 1984
 They are published by the Department of Education & Science and are available from HMSO, London.

3 Solomon J. (1982) 'How children learn about energy, or, Does the First Law come first?' *School Science Review* **63**, **224**, 415–22.

4 Solomon J. (1985) 'Energy for the citizen' in **Energy Matters** (eds. Driver R. & Millar R.). Centre for Studies in Science & Mathematics Education, Leeds University.

5 Claxton G.L. (1985) 'Teaching and acquiring scientific knowledge' in *Kelly in the Classrooms: Educational Aspects of Personal Construct Psychology.* Montreal, Cybersystems, Inc.

6 Millar R. (1987) *Teaching physics as a non-specialist. A survey of the views of teachers without formal physics qualifications.* Department of Education, University of York.

7 For a lengthy and interesting discussion of this issue, see the article 'Beyond processes' by Driver R. & Millar R. (1987) in *Studies in Science Education*, **14**, 32–62.

8 See Chalmers A. (1982) *What is This Thing Called Science?* (2nd ed.) Open University Press, for an interesting and readable account of many of the differences.

9 Smail B. (1984) *Girl-friendly Science: Avoiding Sex Bias in the Curriculum.* Longman Resources Unit, York.

1 Motion

Treatments of this topic generally start by introducing the concept of speed and velocity. Few pupils are aware of the difference between the two and speed is the word that they naturally use. Many of the more traditional introductions lack imagination and the topic often seems dry and abstract. Yet an understanding of the mechanics of movement is central to all physics, which is why the topic is introduced so early. So any initial treatment should point to the plethora of objects that move or are moving. It is well worth trying to arouse a sense of wonder with the world by starting from an astronomical perspective and posing the following questions.

> We live on a world that is round, yet we do not fall off. Many people used to believe the world was flat. Some still do. What evidence is there that it is round?
>
> We believe that the Earth is moving around the Sun but how do we know this? Before Copernicus, most people believed that the Earth was static, and the Sun moved around it.
>
> The Earth moves in a circular orbit and never slows down. Most objects in the world seem to travel in straight lines and slow down. Why is the Earth different?

The point of this is to pose some questions about motion and focus pupils' thinking. It is a good idea to give them the exercise of thinking out what their ideas are. Ask them to imagine that they are Newton and were beginning to write the *Principia*, Newton's great work. What rules of motion would they put in it?

A debate organised around the topic of flat Earth v. round Earth helps them to see that physics is a human activity where hypotheses are tested against the evidence. In everyday life we need to be able to measure how fast a car is going, the flow of blood through the heart and the speed of a runner. The development of modern science and technology started with a better understanding of force and motion based on the ideas of Galileo and Newton.

It is important to challenge long-cherished notions about the world. Most children's ideas are not explicit but intuitive. Using a brick and a small pebble, form the pupils into groups and ask the pupils to discuss which is going to get to the ground first when dropped from the same height. General experience reveals a substantial number who believe that the heavier object will arrive first. Try challenging the strength of this belief by gambling a bar of chocolate on the outcome! It is very unlikely that this will be a severe strain on your pocket!

The result does act as a powerful stimulus to experiment with other objects and to hypothesise as to why some objects do fall at the same rate, taking an equivalent time to reach the ground, and others do not. Pupils could be asked to devise an experiment that would test the effect of the air. The 'Guinea and Feather' experiment should be demonstrated if it has not been suggested by the pupils. This fascinating experiment can be further reinforced by showing a recording[1] of the experiment done on the Moon. The activity can be extended by asking pupils to investigate if an additional lateral motion makes any difference. Pupils are asked to throw one pebble sideways whilst simultaneously dropping another vertically.

Such experiments should lead the class through discussion to the idea that there is a need to be more objective and to measure the speed of the object. Teachers should be aware of the difference between velocity, which is a vector because it has speed *and* direction, and speed which is merely a scalar quantity because it only has size. The definition of velocity is

$$velocity = \frac{change\ of\ displacement}{time}$$

Displacement is a vector in that it represents distance travelled in a specific direction. Distance travelled, which is used in the definition of speed, is a scalar as it only has a magnitude which could be in any direction. Thus speed is defined by

$$speed = \frac{distance\ travelled}{time\ taken}$$

Hence if the distance from London to Birmingham is 150 km and the time taken is 2 hours, then the speed is 75 km/hour. Such a statement says nothing about the direction and also reflects the fact that what is calculated is the average speed. The actual speed will vary considerably in those two hours. Far too often the following is observed

$$velocity = \frac{distance}{time}$$

The error may seem minor, but if language is used loosely by the teacher it is not surprising if the pupils fail to establish a clear understanding of these ideas. All disciplines are a way of knowing and one of the aims of the teacher is to introduce the pupils to the reserved language of the subjects, to attach meanings to words and to explore the excitement of new ways of seeing. Pupils invariably use speed, but as teachers we should attempt to be more rigorous with our vocabulary.

Most introductions lead to the measurement of speed. This is commonly introduced using the ticker timer. This noisy machine acts as a good exemplar of one of the problems of school science, that is the use of specialised pieces of apparatus that are not found elsewhere and that isolate the subject from the real world it purports to be exploring. This is where imagination must be demanded from children. They have jumped aboard Dr Who's Tardis and arrived in the 15th century. How would they attempt to measure the speed of the horse they are travelling on? Again this is best done as an activity in small groups where children discuss possible answers and then present their solutions. Small group work like this provides a chance for children to begin to use the language of physics which aids their understanding.

The teaching sequence can then move to the introduction of the ticker timer as the physics teacher's solution. Essentially it is an ingenious piece of apparatus that measures the distance travelled in successive small time intervals, for which there is no readily available, cheap substitute. At this stage it is necessary to issue a warning to those who would follow the standard treatment in many textbooks and introduce an approach that goes on to develop the equations of motion, *DON'T!*

Precise mathematical formulations of physics inevitably lead to rote learning, even amongst the brightest pupils. There is little chance that average pupils will then be able to relate abstract graphs to any form of qualitative experience they have and this is essentially what the ticker timer is good at doing. A qualitative treatment helps to focus on concepts and their association which is the prime aim of an introductory treatment. In addition, the recurring physics teachers' nightmare is likely to be experienced: that is the lack of any mathematical confidence in 13–14 year old pupils. It would be unfair to blame the maths teacher. The level of maths we expect is often quite sophisticated. Also it is important to realise that modern maths courses may approach equations in a different way to the formalism employed by most science teachers. Appendix 1 provides a fuller discussion of this.

A much better treatment is to combine the introduction to the subject with a substantial amount of practical work and demonstrations with a lot of discussion of the results and graphs. Graphs can be made of pupils walking, objects falling and running down inclined slopes. The statement 'Every picture tells a story' is one that is very applicable to graphs. They are records that provide information, and practice in their construction and interpretation is important if pupils are to build a sound understanding. This will take time. However, since much of this work is essential for later progress, it is pointless rushing on like a tourist doing a 10-day tour of Europe, seeing all and experiencing nothing. Later, it is important that children appreciate that the slope of a distance–time graph is a measure of the speed of an object while the area under a speed–time graph is equivalent to the distance travelled.

A preliminary introduction to the topic will have achieved a substantial amount if it has covered an understanding of speed, velocity and velocity–time graphs, Newton's First Law and the independence of gravitational acceleration from mass. From this most GCSE candidates will be expected to develop a knowledge and understanding of all Newton's laws, acceleration and momentum (this is now optional in many syllabuses), all of which have a number of differences.

Newton's Laws

The First Law

To many teachers this seems the simplest of all concepts in Newtonian mechanics. Yet in many ways it is the most difficult to accept. Gunstone & Watts (1986)[2] have reviewed the research findings and identified five intuitive rules that are commonly held by pupils:
- forces are to do with living things;
- constant motion requires constant force;
- the amount of motion is proportional to the amount of force;
- if a body is not moving there is no force on it;
- if a body is moving, there is a force acting on it in the direction of motion.

These are, of course, based on childrens' everyday perception of the world, but from the scientific viewpoint all are fallacious. Many of these can be described as Aristotelian concepts or are similar to Buridan's impetus theory which was that a moving object has an internal source of 'impetus' which it was given when first thrown or moved. A proper understanding of Newton's First Law challenges all these notions. These alternative concepts act as an obstacle to understanding. It would be presumptuous to believe that the superficial introduction to this found in many physics texts[3] will effectively dislodge these notions.

All that is commonly done in physics lessons to demonstrate our firmly held belief in Newton's First Law is to demonstrate the idea with carbon dioxide or air pucks on a glass table or to use a linear air track, both of which mimimise the effect of friction so that it is barely perceptible. Even so, neither of these demonstrations would really convince the normal sceptical audience of a group of 14 year olds. It is important to challenge pupils' views with more convincing evidence than this and make them realise that their intuitive ideas are not successful at explaining observations in a variety of situations. A useful stimulus for discussion is many of the videos that are available of motion in Space.[4] The question then should be posed as to why objects in Space keep going at constant velocity with no external force applied while those around us do not. Another example which can be used which is more likely to be part of the pupil's everyday experience is motion on an ice rink or on roller skates. This could be used to form the basis of a physics trip. There are also available several computer programs[5,6] that provide microworlds which allow the pupils to explore a Newtonian environment from the basis of a game. Papert[7] and di Sessa[8] have argued that such microworlds provide a dynamical environment that allows true heuristic discovery to take place. Figure 1.1 shows the screen from one of these. The pupil can apply thrusts in the horizontal and vertical directions, switch gravity and friction on and off independently and add a trace to illustrate the motion.

With the use of the structured materials accompanying them, such programs help to illustrate that the dynamics of objects on the surface of the Earth are affected by the presence of a gravitational field and friction. The program

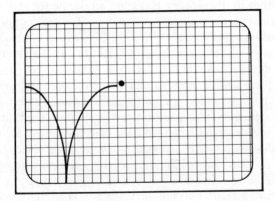

1.1 Screen from computer program exploring Newton's laws

also comes with several microworlds where the rules governing the motion are not explicit and pupils are asked to explore and discover the rules governing the dynamics in these microworlds. There is no definitive evidence to point to the success of such materials as yet. However, it is quite clear that present methods are not succeeding and that new avenues need to be explored.

The Second Law

This is traditionally taught with two experiments that involve accelerating trolleys with elastics[9]. These are one set of experiments where it is essential to have the manufacturer's elastics. Substitutes tend to accelerate the trolleys and accompanying pupils to velocities where something dangerous happens to either the child or the equipment. The runways used in this experiment should be 'friction compensated' and, even then, do not expect to obtain results that clearly support Newton's Second Law. The apparatus is not sophisticated and there are many simple sources of error, such as the difficulty of maintaining a constant force and missing dots. However, summarising the class results in a table like table 1.1 on the board will allow wildly erroneous results to be discarded, and generally there are sufficient results to confirm the idea that *doubling the force, doubles the acceleration and tripling the force, triples the acceleration* (provided the mass is constant).

Table 1.1

Force (no. of elastics)	1	2	3
Acceleration (cm/tt²)*	1.1	2.5	3.4
	1.5	2.2	3.7
	0.9	2.0	2.0
Average	1.16	2.23	3.33

*See appendix 3 on units

There is no point in doing this experiment, however, if it is merely being used to confirm theory, since it is not likely to be a great success and leaves pupils

13

with the impression that 'if it's physics, it doesn't work'. Better methods of demonstrating this are available with devices like the VELA and are discussed later. The only real justification for doing this as a class experiment is that it provides an opportunity to develop manipulative skills in handling apparatus and performing quantitative calculations.

Before performing these experiments, though, it is necessary to teach how we measure acceleration. Discussion should reveal that most pupils have an intuitive concept of acceleration as being 'how fast something speeds up'. The basic difficulty is that the idea to be explained is the measurement of the rate of change of velocity, that is, *the rate of change of a rate*. If an object has an acceleration of 5 m/s², then this means that in every second, the velocity increases by 5 m/s, so that acceleration is measured by the change in velocity each second. It is best to start with the familiar: if a bicycle accelerates from 0 to 20 miles per hour in 10 seconds, this means that it changes its speed by 2 miles per hour every second. This we would call an acceleration of 2 miles per hour per second. If a walker accelerates from standing to 4 m/s in 2 secs, then this is an acceleration of 2 m/s per second which we write as 2 m/s². Here the simple numbers provide a convenient hook onto which abstract concepts can be latched. Inevitably pupils need formulae here as crutches to assist them while the concept develops, and these should be provided.

Acceleration is normally introduced from ticker tape graphs where velocities have been measured in cm/ten-tick (cm/tt). These are very definitely non-SI units but are deliberately chosen for ease of mathematical manipulation[10].

The normal line of argument would be to take a suitable 5 ten-tick period off the graph and ask how much the velocity has increased by. In Figure 1.2 this

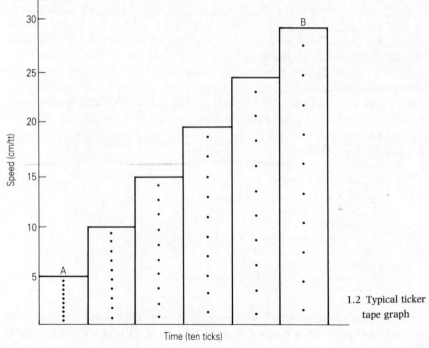

1.2 Typical ticker tape graph

would be done by measuring the velocity at A (5 cm in 1 ten-tick), then measuring the velocity at B, 5 ten-ticks later, which is 30 cm in 1 ten-tick and advancing the following argument.

Velocity at B = 30 cm/tt
velocity at A = 5 cm/tt
increase in velocity   = 25 cm/tt in 5 ten-ticks
increase in velocity *in one ten-tick*   = 5 cm/tt in 1 tt
which can be written as   = 5 cm/tt/tt
but by standard practice is written as = 5 cm/tt^2.

The next step is to show how to convert ten-ticks to seconds so that the increase is in cm/s^2 (multiply by 25) and then to convert the distance to metres. Although this is long-winded and the units of ten-ticks for time are totally arbitrary inventions of the science laboratory, this is one case where such a development provides a more accessible route to an understanding of the concepts involved. A useful tutorial aid that provides a clear audio-visual explanation of many of the ideas underlying velocity–time graphs and the measurement of acceleration by combining computer software with broadcast material is published by the BBC[11].

The other difficult idea being introduced is that of proportion. This abstract mathematical concept involving understanding of ratio is only achieved by pupils who become 'formal thinkers' in Piagetian terms. Shayer & Adey[12] have shown that many children do not achieve such a stage of thinking till later. Hence the topic must be approached with care and empathy. Pupils do not spend their time in mathematics any longer doing problems of the kind 'if it takes six men two hours to dig a ditch, how long does it take one? However from examples such as table 1.1, they will be able to say that there is a pattern, which can be stated in terms of the outcome of doubling or tripling one variable.

Examples from other areas are often useful and the Nuffield Physics course[13] provides a useful illustration of the calculation of the cost of painting a wall. This is directly proportional to the height and directly proportional to the length, and the cost/m^2 is the constant that relates area to cost

$$\text{cost} = \text{cost/m}^2 \times \text{length} \times \text{height}$$

However, rather than introducing the pupils to the complexities of proportion, it is much simpler to state that such a pattern is what is called a proportional relationship which is expressed as

$$a \propto F$$

where a is the acceleration and F is the force.

The second experiment which is done using the same number of elastics (preferably two) produces a table of results like that in table 1.2

Table 1.2

Mass of trolley	1	2	3
Acceleration (cm/tt²)	10	4	3
	12	5	2
	9	6	4
Average	10.33	5	3

Discussion of the pattern that these figures show should reveal that '*doubling the mass halves the acceleration, tripling the mass reduces the acceleration by a third*'. Again this provides an intuitive feel for the relationship. The mathematical expression is

$$a \propto \frac{1}{m}$$

where *m* is mass.

These two proportional equations can be combined to give

$$a = \frac{F}{m}$$

or by rearrangement

$$F = ma$$

The numbers work out correctly because this equation is used to define what is meant by a force of 1 newton. Hence by internationally agreed convention

$$1 \text{ newton} = 1 \text{ kg} \times 1 \text{ m/s}^2.$$

This may be glossing over some of the deeper significance of the mathematical manipulations, but pupils seem to find it more acceptable than the fuller explanation which confuses rather than simplifies. There are many more examples in later years to teach what is meant by proportion.

This approach to teaching Newton's Second Law has been challenged by the introduction of modern devices such as the VELA[14]. This is one example of the microprocessor-based instrumentation now available to the teacher of physics which is discussed further in chapter 10. Fitted with the physics EPROM[15] and a light sensor, it is possible to measure the acceleration of an object directly.

Fig. 1.3 shows one arrangement of the apparatus. The trolley is accelerated by a load attached to the string at the other end. This load can be a 100 g (1 N force), then 200 g and 300 g. The instrument is fed with the dimensions of the card on the trolley and times how long the beam is intercepted by the first section, for which it calculates the velocity. It repeats this for the second section

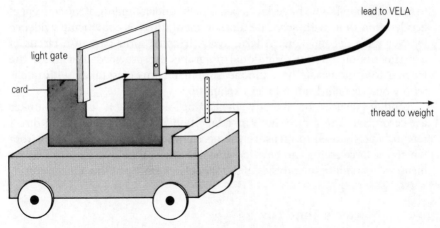

1.3 Arrangement of trolley and light sensor to use with VELA

and then calculates the acceleration. Many values for acceleration at each force can rapidly be taken and the values averaged. Typical results are shown in fig. 1.4.

This experiment provides more satisfactory evidence[16] for the validity of Newton's Second Law and avoids the necessity to understand exactly how acceleration is measured in the first method. This may best be done as a demonstration

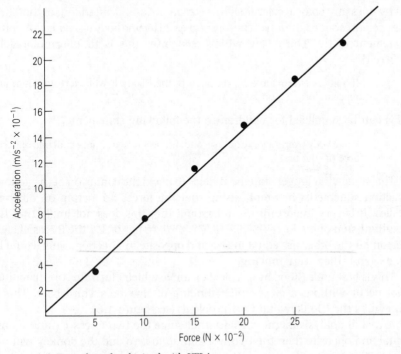

1.4 Typical results obtained with VELA

to convince pupils who have developed a 'tacit' understanding of the concept of acceleration that, with accurate measurement, there is convincing evidence for Newton's Second Law. Alternatively, it could form part of a circus of experiments on motion. Additional programs are provided that allow the teacher to demonstrate how the measurements are being taken with pupils who would benefit from a fuller explanation.

Another device for directly measuring acceleration is the Bunker accelerometer. This is essentially an adaptation of the spirit level, but its direct reading can be used to measure the acceleration of cars and bicycles from which the force acting can be calculated if the mass is known. This provides a means of extending the physics of the school laboratory to the outside world.

Newton's Third Law

The difficulty with the idea here is a result of the rather unhelpful way in which this law is often phrased. The following is a list of popular versions often seen in textbooks.

○ 'Every action has an equal and opposite reaction.'
○ 'To every force there is an equal and opposite force.'
○ 'Action and reaction are equal and opposite.'

Such formulations cause inevitable confusion with the conditions for equilibrium as it conjures up the idea of two forces acting in opposite directions adding up to give a net zero resultant force which begs the logical question 'Why does any body accelerate if this is true?'. An understanding of the Third Law requires a recognition of the forces exerted by one body *on another*. A better statement of the Third Law which recognises this is that formulated by Warren[17].

> 'If body A exerts force F_A on body B, then body B will exert an equal and opposite force F_B on body A.'

This can be simplified for children to the following statement.

> 'If one body exerts a force on a second, the second exerts an equal and opposite force on the first.'

This somewhat longer statement helps to avoid the confusion of the action–reaction statements by emphasising that the forces are acting on different bodies. It is very important to understand that this does not imply that the resultant sum of the forces *on one body* is zero. In figure 1.5 the forces of each person on the other are equal in size and opposite in direction. This would be true even if they were moving.

This is best understood by a typical example which illustrates the difficulties that occur without a clear understanding of Newton's Third Law. This is known as the 'Donkey and Cart problem' (see figure 1.6).

A casual analysis might consider that since the two forces F_A and F_B are equal and opposite then the two will add up to zero and the donkey will not move. This is patently absurd. However, whether the cart moves depends on the net force acting on it. The two forces acting on the cart are F_A and the

18

F_A the force of Tom on Anne
F_B the force of Anne on Tom

Anne   Tom

1.5 Forces acting on two bodies

1.6 Forces acting on donkey and cart

frictional force F_f. Whether the cart accelerates depends only on whether F_A is greater than F_f. It it is, then the cart will accelerate in the direction of the resultant force.

The problem with the popular statements of Newton's Third Law is that they do not make explicit what the forces are acting on. The implicit but mistaken assumption is that it is the same object. Anybody with this idea would have difficulty explaining why the cart moved.

Mass

This can be defined as the quantity of matter in a body. Since the amount of matter is invariant regardless of where the object is, then the mass of an object should not change. The standard mass is still defined in terms of a lump of platinum kept in Paris and this is the 1 kg mass to which all others are ultimately compared.

Masses are measured by comparing one mass with another of known mass. This can be done by applying an equivalent force to each and comparing the accelerations produced, or by comparing the gravitational force on two masses. In the school laboratory, the former method is demonstrated with what is known as an inertial balance, more commonly rechristened 'the wig-wag machine' (figure 1.7).

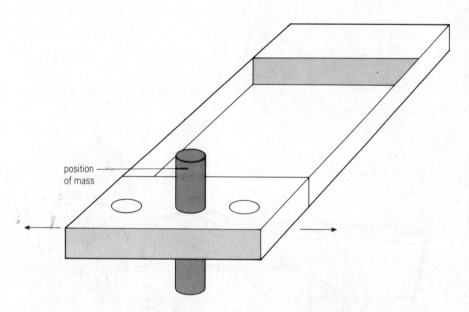

position of mass

1.7 Wig-wag machine

The standard force is applied by displacing the arm to one side. The rate of oscillation is dependent *only on mass* and not weight. Adding more masses reduces the period of oscillation but supporting the weight of the mass with a long string makes no difference to the rate of oscillation. Hence the matter still has mass which has inertia. These are difficult ideas involving a subtle but important distinction. Do not be surprised if children find it hard to grasp and it may be advisable to omit it with a less-able class.

The other method uses a beam balance (figure 1.8). This compares the gravitational mass. If the masses are equal, the gravitational force (mg-mass × gravitational field strength) on mass A is the same as that on mass B and the beam will balance.

It does not matter where the balance is on the Earth or on the Moon for instance, as the gravitational field strength g is identical for both of the masses. In earlier days, this used to cause confusion because the chemists would use such devices for 'weighing' chemicals when they were really comparing their mass with standard masses. However, the advent of modern digital balances

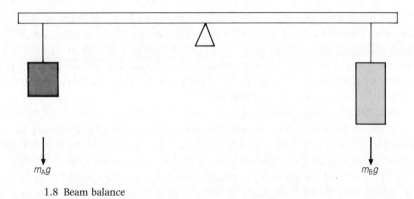

1.8 Beam balance

has now consigned these devices to the high street antique shop. Digital balances use an ingenious equivalent of a spring and hence are devices for 'weighing' and measuring the force of gravity on an object.

Weight

The weight of a body is usually defined in terms of the force of gravity acting on it. If one accepts this definition without reservation for the moment, this means that the weight of a body is equal to its mass multiplied by the gravitational field strength, i.e. mg, and is measured in newtons, generally with a spring balance. Since the gravitational field strength varies according to where you are in space, the weight of a body will also vary. You would not weigh the same on the Moon as you do on Earth. It is important to realise that this definition does not mean that astronauts in orbit around the Earth are weightless as the astronauts are still in a gravitational field. They may appear to be weightless but this is because both the astronauts and the spacecraft are in orbit around the Earth being accelerated towards the centre all the time by the force of gravity. This means that they are both falling with the same acceleration so anybody in the spacecraft 'experiences' the sensation of weightlessness. The same sensation would be experienced by any individual in a lift where the cable had just broken. A small push off the floor would cause the individual to accelerate towards the top.

However, in terms of the definition of weight given above, orbiting astronauts do have weight. The intuitive response of pupils is that the astronauts are weightless. Quite naturally this idea is difficult for pupils to accept, partly because many pupils believe that the astronauts have been shot so high that there is no gravity where they are. This point alone is worth exploring with pupils by discussion of how far out gravity works. When they have arrived at their conclusion ask 'What keeps the Moon in orbit?' The problem for astronauts who stay in Space for some time, is how to monitor their mass and discover whether they are 'putting on or losing weight'. The solution used in the Spacelab was to arrange a large version or a wig-wag balance with the astronaut sitting in a chair. When the astronaut put on mass, the oscillation became slower.

You experience the sensation of weight because when you stand on the floor the floor pushes back on you to stop you falling through. This sensation, of the floor pushing back, is what people tend to call their weight. Some authors have defined weight as 'the force exerted on a body by its support'. In terms of this definition then astronauts would be 'weightless' as there is no force exerted on them by their support, the spacecraft.

Both definitions have problems, the former suffers from the fact that the force on a spring balance is not always the same as the force of gravity due to the rotation of the Earth. However the difference is only 0.3% at the equator. The latter suffers from the problem that it really requires an understanding of Newton's Third Law and statics to be understood and used effectively by pupils. It would also mean that high jumpers and divers are weightless which is difficult for pupils to accept. Most teachers and curriculum materials define weight as the force of gravity on an object because it is simpler and more readily understood. This means that astronauts in orbit still have weight but they just don't experience it! The BBC produced an excellent television programme on the topic called *Free Fall*[1] in their series *Science Topics* which discusses the whole issue. Another excellent demonstration and discussion of the issues is found in the programme Gravity[4] in the *Scientific Eye* series. Both are highly recommended for pupils and teachers.

Measurement of weight

In terms of the accepted definition, the weight of an object is the force on it. This means that we should measure weight with spring balances calibrated in newtons. Unfortunately life is not as simple as this. All our weighing machines at home are calibrated in units of mass such as grammes and, even worse, ounces, pounds and stones. How does the poor teacher reconcile this apparent conflict? This is not easy, but essentially you have to tell your pupils that the greengrocer is guilty of deception. The force on a 1 kg mass here on the surface of the Earth is approximately 10 N. Because newtons are not part of our everyday language, the greengrocer decided to call the 10 N weight a 1 kg weight and is misusing the terms as 1 kg is a unit of mass and not a unit of weight. However the problem is intractable, rather like changing over to driving on the right, we cannot change all the balances that exist. Teachers should feel a measure of success if their pupils understand that they would not get the same mass of potatoes on the Moon as a 1 kg mass does not weigh the same on the Moon; though it does have the same mass, as the amount of matter contained in it has not changed at all.

Momentum

The momentum of a body is the *mass* multiplied by the *velocity* and has units of kg m/s. Why is momentum so fundamental to physics? Knowing the answer to this question helps the teacher confronted with teaching the subject. Essentially much physics is about the dynamics of objects. The conservation of the total momentum of a system in any interactions is one of the dynamical principles which is applied to the interaction between objects to predict their behaviour. At the microscopic level, an understanding of momentum helped the development of the kinetic theory and to explain the pressure exerted by gases. Nowadays it is fundamental to interpreting the result of nuclear scattering experiments that have led to a better understanding of matter. On the macroscopic level, an understanding of momentum enables the effective design of seat belts, crash barriers and safer cars.

There are essentially two views about the teaching of momentum. The first is that momentum is an abstract formal concept with units that have no readily accessible meaning and hence is difficult for pupils to comprehend. It is notable that it is now specifically excluded from many GCSE syllabuses for this reason. In the traditional approach, pupils need to develop an intuitive sense of the behaviour of simple objects in collisions before being introduced to the formal physics. Thus examples with billiard balls, trolleys of similar and different masses and collisions between pupils on skateboards or skates help to raise questions about the possibility of predicting the behaviour of objects involved in collisions. The concept of momentum and its measurement can then be introduced. Pupils can be posed the challenge of investigating how it varies in a collision.

However several authors[18] have argued recently for a more radical approach to dynamics starting from momentum and momentum flow. Their argument is that children already hold the intuitive view that objects move forward because 'there is something in them which keeps them going'. Such an approach would capitalise on this misconception to introduce the study of force by talking about moving objects and the 'something' in them which keeps them going, calling this 'momentum', and then considering what it is that causes changes in momentum. This would introduce the term 'force' for pushes and pulls which act on objects to change momentum and lead to an appreciation that a net resultant force acting on a body will cause a change in momentum. An extension of this argument says that the teaching of many situations in physics always starts with the steady state, for example objects with constant velocity, currents that do not change. Children do not relate to this as there is a lack of causality about it. What brought the object into the state of motion? What causes the current to be steady? To start with intuitive concepts of motion and look at what causes changes would be more sensible to the natural understanding of children.

Later work would introduce the measuring of momentum and show that changes in momentum can be measured by multiplying force and time of contact. This is called 'impulse'. This is done by accelerating a trolley with a constant force for a known period of time and measuring the momentum at the end. This should show the following relationship

$$\text{change in momentum} = \text{force} \times \text{time} = \text{impulse}$$

Experiments that can be done in the laboratory show that changes in momentum for objects in collisions and explosions are equal and opposite. That is, one object's gain is another object's loss[19]. The experiments consist of using trolleys and ticker timers to measure the velocity of objects before and after

23

collisions. These take some care and pupils often have difficulty in identifying the point of collision on the tape. It can then be argued that, since the time of contact is the same for both objects and the changes in momentum are equal and opposite, the force of contact must be equal in size and in opposite directions. This approach is taken in the SCISP course[20] and has been used successfully by Osborne & Freyberg[21].

Momentum applications generally consist of problems of protecting people when they are involved in collisions with other objects, often the ground or car dashboards. In all these situations the person has a certain quantity of momentum which they must transfer. This is done by the body applying an impulse to the ground or the dashboard. Human bodies do not withstand large forces, so it is essential to transfer the momentum by applying a small force for a comparatively long time. For this reason car dashboards are designed from materials that will yield slowly, thus extending the time of contact and reducing the force exerted on the body. People jumping to the ground bend their knees instinctively to extend the time of contact during which their momentum changes and reduce the force exerted by the legs. Consequently this reduces the force of the ground on their legs (by Newton's Third Law) which minimises the possibility of fracture. This is simply and convincingly demonstrated by asking a pupil to jump off a bench!

One problem that can cause difficulties for the inexperienced is the bright spark of a pupil who asks where their momentum comes from when they start walking. After all they had no momentum before and now they seem to have mysteriously gained some. The answer to this is that they had to accelerate themselves by pressing back on the Earth. In doing so they gave the Earth an equal but opposite momentum backwards so that the net change is zero. This may sound absurd but it's true. Of course, the Earth is much heavier than the average pupil so the acceleration is effectively zero. However, if all the Chinese started walking East they would accelerate the world in a westerly direction.

Finally, this is the opportunity to enliven the whole topic by a short treatment of rockets, either in terms of momentum or Newton's Third Law. The treatment of rockets is best introduced by illustrating that most objects on the Earth require something to push against to commence moving. Yet out in Space there is nothing to push against, so how does a rocket manage to accelerate? Pupils can then be asked to consider the momentum changes and see how this would help to explain what is happening, which provides them with an opportunity to come to their own understanding of the topic before the teacher provides the explanation.

The real fun of rockets though is the experiments and demonstrations that can be done. The action of a rocket can be demonstrated with a sparklets bulb attached to a trolley and pierced with a nail. Firework rockets can be shown and demonstrated safely outside. Opening one reveals the small nozzle through which the exhaust gases exit. Gunpowder is a very effective fuel because the sulphur and carbon react with the oxidant, potassium chlorate, to produce gases which escape at high velocity from the rear. The rocket gains an equal but opposite forward momentum. Igniting the gunpowder in an exposed space shows this clearly. It is well worth investing in a small piece of apparatus that converts old plastic lemonade bottles into water rockets[22]. The rockets use water as fuel which is ejected by compressed air which has been pumped in with a footpump.

This demonstration requires some space but is one generally much enjoyed by all. It can be extended for those with large playing fields into investigations of the acceleration of the rocket which can be measured with a ticker timer. Pupils could be given the open-ended problem of investigating what factors decide the height achieved. They will need to devise a method of measuring the height and could look at the variation with the quantity of fuel and the pressure of the gas.

Circular motion

Yet again, the difficulty with the subject is that the pedagogical message the teacher has to introduce contradicts intuitive experience. The physical explanation of why an object moves in a circle is that there is a centripetal force towards the centre. That this must be so is evident from a brief thought about the motion of the Moon. The Moon moves in a circle around the Earth. A brief discussion of what stops it flying off into Space should lead to the suggestion from the pupils that gravity is the force acting and that it pulls the Moon towards the centre of the Earth.

However, anybody's experience of swinging a bung or a conker on a piece of string is that of an outward force on their finger. Similarly, the fairground machines which bear a resemblance to large spin driers seem to fling you against the side and the force at work seems to be an outward force, the so-called 'centrifugal force'. This is such a common misconception that popular science and advertising often use the term 'centrifugal force' to explain the effects of many rotating machines. Chemists using a machine called a 'centri-fuge' and industry using a technique called 'centrifugal casting' are two of the many examples.

Pupils' experience of rotating a bung on a string is that there is a force acting away from the centre. This is true, but it is not the force acting on the bung. This perception leads to the notion that when the string is released in the former example the object will fly out from the circle because of the force acting. A clear understanding of the situation is dependent upon a good comprehension of Newton's Third Law and First Law. A correct explanation of the two initial examples would be as follows.

(a) *Bung on a string*. The force the pupil experiences is a force on their finger and not a force on the bung/conker. Because forces come in pairs, there is an equal and opposite force on the bung/conker which is directed towards the centre, that is the centripetal force. When the force is removed, the object continues in a straight line as predicted by Newton's First Law. The best demonstration for this is to swing a bung around your head at the front of the class and ask the pupils where you should let go in order to hit them (see figure 1.9). Most will suggest somewhere between position A and B. In reality, you must let go when it is at C.

This simple experiment is another one that challenges well-established alternative concepts of children. The children should be given an opportunity

25

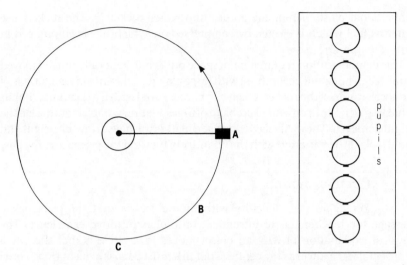

1.9 Demonstration of forces acting in circular motion

to try the experiment themselves, preferably outside, and then discuss in small groups why the bung does not go where they predicted. Only after the children are dissatisfied with their ideas should the teacher attempt to introduce the concept of centripetal force and remind the pupils of Newton's First Law.

(b) *The fairground machine.* In these machines the individual stands with their back to the circular wall. The machine then starts to rotate at a comparatively high velocity and a hydraulic ram tilts the circular drum to an angle of 70–80°. Despite this, the individual does not fall out, though it does not do much for the sense of balance. The force the individual experiences is due to the fact that the wall presses on their back in order to make them go round in a circle. Because an individual has mass and hence inertia, they press on the wall with an equal and opposite force and this sensation is interpreted as being 'flung out'. Again teachers with the time and access to a fairground locally might consider a trip to demonstrate some of these ideas!

The conclusion that we are aiming for children to draw is that the real force making an object move in a circle is a force towards the centre of the circle which we call a centripetal force. It is often helpful to explain the origins of such words in order to remember the concept. 'Centripetal' is a good example in that it is a combination of two Latin words, *centrum* for the centre and *peto* meaning 'to go in', that is to go into the centre. Physics is full of words of Latin and Greek origin which a good dictionary will explain. Some pupils find technical words easy to remember if the etymology of the words is explained.

All these problems do not make life easy for the physics teacher. Jon Ogborn[23] has summarised the pupil's difficulties with Newton's laws of motion as

   ○ the first law is unbelievable;
   ○ the second law is incomprehensible;
   ○ the third law is merely religious incantation.

This may be a rather extreme interpretation of their problems, but it points effectively to the difficulties of teaching mechanics and the ease with which these can be underestimated. It is worth remembering that what is being attempted in the science laboratory in five years took society considerably longer to accept. Koyré[24] gives the following statement.

> 'What the founders of modern science, among them Galileo, had to do, was not to criticise and combat certain faulty theories, but to replace them by better ones. They had to do something quite different. They had to destroy one world and to replace it by another. They had to reshape the framework of our intellect itself, to restate and reform its concepts, to evolve a new approach to being, a new concept of knowledge, a new concept of science – and even to replace a pretty natural approach, that of common sense, by another which is not natural at all.'

This then is the task confronting the teacher of physics.

Notes and references

1 *Free Fall*. BBC (1984) Science Topic Series.
2 Gunstone R. & Watts M. (1986) in *Children's Ideas in Science* (eds. Driver R., Guesne E. & Tiberghien A.) Open University Press, Milton Keynes.
3 For example see Duncan T. (1986) *GCSE Physics*. John Murray, London.
4 *Gravity*. Scientific Eye series. Yorkshire TV.
5 *Mobile*. Science in Process Software, Capital Media, ILECC, John Ruskin St, London SE5.
6 *Newtonian Games* is a computer-assisted learning package available from Longmans, 1986.
7 Papert S. (1980) *Mindstorms*. Harvester Press, Brighton.
8 di Sessa A. (1982), 'Unlearning Aristotelian concepts in motion.' *Cognitive Science*, **6**, 37–75.
9 For a fairly standard approach to the teaching of Newton's Second Law, see *Teachers' Guide, Year IV, Revised Nuffield Physics* (1981) Longmans, Harlow.
10 See appendix 3 for a fuller discussion of units.
11 *Uniformly Accelerated Motion*. (1986) BBC Software. BBC Publications.
12 Shayer M. & Adey P. (1981) *Towards a Science of Science Teaching*. Heinemann, London.
13 *Teachers' Guide, Year IV, Revised Nuffield Physics* (1981) pages 25–8, Longmans, Harlow.
14 VELA (Versatile Laboratory Aid) manufactured by Data Harvest Ltd, 28 Lake St, Leighton Buzzard, Bedfordshire.
15 Physics EPROM. This is a chip which increases the range of measurements possible by the VELA. It is available from Instrumentation Software Ltd, 7 Gledhow Avenue, Leeds LS8 1NY.
16 The results from this experiment are only valid if the masses used to provide the accelerating force are much smaller than the accelerating mass. This means that two trolleys should be used as the mass which is accelerated. This was the original reason for introducing elastics to accelerate the masses in the Nuffield experiments.
In addition, it should be pointed out that this experiment relies on that which it is trying to prove, since the value of the force accelerating the trolley is calculated by applying Newton's Second Law. However this is a subtle point which very few pupils are remotely capable of spotting. Since the experiment is so simple and straightforward to perform, and apparently convincing to pupils, there are good educational grounds for using it even if the physics may be suspect.
17 Warren J. (1979) *Understanding Force*. Butterworths, London.

18 di Sessa A.A. (1980) 'Momentum flow, an alternative perspective in elementary mechanics.' *American Journal of Physics* **48**, no. 5, 365–9.
19 It is important to remember here that momentum is a vector quantity and equal changes in momentum in opposite directions will have opposite signs.
20 SCISP (Schools Council Integrated Science Project), *Book 3: Energy, Teacher's guide* (1972) Longmans, Harlow.
21 Osborne R. & Freyberg P. (1985) *Learning in Science*. Heinemann, London.
22 This kit which costs approximately £10 is available from Hinterland Ltd, Rokit Dept, Mill Green, Hatfield, Herts, AL19 SN2.
23 Ogborn J. (1983) 'Difficulties in dynamics.' *Physics at Secondary School: Physics and Applications Vol. II. Proceedings for the Conference 1983*. Institute of Physics, Slovak Academy of Sciences.
24 Koyré A. (1943) *Journal of Historical Ideas*, **4**, **400**, p. 405.

2 Energy

Energy is one of the basic ideas used in all scientific disciplines. Science education must attempt to give children an understanding of this fundamental concept. The difficulty for physics teachers is that children arrive in the classroom with an understanding of the word which is generated by their experiences of everyday life. Very often, this is inconsistent with the scientific view. There is another similar problem for teachers since the physicist's specialised interpretation of the word is often not the same as that used by biology and chemistry teachers. Other curriculum areas are also using the theme of energy for historical and sociological treatments of issues in society. The consequence is that there are multiple meanings for the word 'energy' and this if often exacerbated by a lack of clarity and understanding amongst physics and science teachers.

How can these difficulties be reconciled? Energy has at least three different sets of concepts associated with it: the strict thermodynamic concept, the simplified concept that we teach in school, and the whole range of alternative conceptions in use by children (and teachers!). Because of this, the scientific concept of energy is widely misunderstood and often wrongly used. Most of this chapter is devoted to discussing these varied meanings, their implications and appropriate ways of discussing energy with pupils.

The meanings of the word 'energy' associated with the different contexts in which students might meet and use it can cause severe difficulties. For instance, in a non-physics context it is quite permissible to say the following

> 'He's lazy – he's got no energy!'
> or 'Energy is what makes things move.'
> or 'The cooker supplies lots of heat energy.'

But in physics these statements are either incorrect or incomplete. In the first example 'energy' is being used in a non-physics sense and given animate properties. The second example is wrong in that energy is not responsible for moving objects, pushes and pulls are; the third example carries an implication of heat as being a separate and distinctive kind of energy, revives notions of 'caloric' and implies that energy is a substance. Unfortunately it is easy to find such statements in many elementary textbooks.

The confusion in physics is made worse by the subtleties of the physics concept, shown by the apparent paradox in this remark.

> 'My physics teacher told me that energy cannot be destroyed – but the government says there is an energy crisis. They can't both be right!'

What *is* energy?

It is essential for teachers of physics to have at the back of their minds a clear view of the scientific answer to this question. They also need to have a feel for the main ideas about energy that we would like children to know and understand. How can such ideas help a child to make better sense of their experience of the world? How can these ideas explain the apparent paradox that energy is supposed to be conserved yet we worry about saving it? For a child's everyday experience gives the distinct impression that energy is not conserved. Electricity and petrol is 'used up' and must constantly be replenished. The key scientific ideas can be summarised as follows.

(1) Energy is conserved

In all processes energy is conserved. There is the same amount of energy after as before an event. Energy conservation essentially *limits* what is possible. Something cannot happen where the total energy is more after the event than before, for instance, a roller coaster cannot end up higher than it started. More importantly though, energy is not the cause of any process and to say that something happens because it has energy is wrong. Energy merely *defines the limits of the possibilities*. This means that statements of the form

'Energy is the "go" of things'

are incorrect and should be avoided. A more appropriate statement would be that energy is needed to lift a weight or to set a car in motion. Without a source of energy these processes cannot happen.

(2) Energy is transferred

There are essentially only two kinds of energy, potential energy which is stored in a 'spring-like' manner and kinetic energy which is a property of moving objects. An object gains potential energy, for instance, when the Earth and the object are moved further apart, effectively stretching the invisible spring between them. In any process or event, energy is transferred between these forms by pushing or pulling. So the child that winds up a toy is *transferring* energy to the spring which is *stored* as potential energy.

Therefore it is acceptable to say that 'cornflakes have energy' in that energy is stored in the chemical bonds of the cornflakes. However, this is really a simplification as the release and transfer of that energy requires more than just the cornflakes as the energy is released by a process of combination with oxygen. So really, the energy is stored and localised in the fuel–oxygen system. Such systems are stores of concentrated energy which can be used to do work.

In all this, there is no need to make any statement about forms of energy other than to say whether it is stored energy or kinetic energy, particularly if the emphasis is placed on the transfer. Heating an object with a gas burner is merely a process of transferring energy from the fuel and oxygen to the water in the pan. The transfer in energy raises its temperature. The idea of 'heat' energy can and should be avoided.

30

The view of energy that emerges is that it is a constant quantity which can be localised and transferred from thing to thing. In an informal sense, it may acceptably be viewed as a 'substance', commodity or quasi-material-like substance.

A very good analogy within limitations is the comparison with money[1]. Cash, credit cards, cheques, bankers drafts, all have purchasing power and are 'forms' of money. However, there is no real difference between them. A £100 cheque has the same value as £100 of cash. On a simplistic economic assumption, the total quantity of money is conserved and there are banks and individuals who store money. The amount of money any one individual or institution owns defines the limits of what is possible. Only when money is transferred from one store to another does something appear to happen.

It is very common in school science and in physics examinations to talk about forms of energy. So when a battery lights a lamp, a typical description would be to say that

chemical energy (in the battery)→electrical energy (in the wires)→light energy

This is incorrect as it implies that there are many different forms of energy which are intrinsically different. There are *not*. There are only two different 'forms of energy', stored energy and kinetic energy. To name 'forms of energy' becomes for most children a process of attaching labels to changes which does not provide an explanation or aid understanding. It also gives the misleading impression that there is something different about energy depending whether it is 'light energy' or 'spring energy' or 'heat energy'. The energy is the same in all cases. Adams[2] gives a good illustration of what is meant when he says

> 'If a woman pays a cheque for £10 into the bank, and the man at the next counter draws out £10 in cash, we do not say that the woman has given the man £10 or that her cheque has been changed into cash. But it does make sense to say that £10 has been transferred, via the bank, from one person to the other. One person has £10 less in her hand, the other person £10 more in his hand and the amount in the bank has not changed.'

So it is with energy, it is merely transferred from one location to another and the total quantity remains the same.

A common view about energy is that it is difficult to teach because it is an abstract accounting quantity. This is not true as energy behaves as if it had inertia and, since mass is a measure of inertia, energy has mass[3]. It is no more sensible to treat energy as an abstraction than to treat money as an abstraction. We manage to educate children about simple issues to do with money so we should be able to do the same with energy.

In all this discussion of energy, it is not necessary to use the word 'heat' except in an informal sense. Heating is a process of transferring energy from one object to another and nothing more. It is not necessary to speak about the object 'having heat energy'.

(3) Energy 'spreads out'

This idea is the basis of the Second Law of thermodynamics which carries a rather strange mystique because it is regarded as something very difficult. In actual fact it is a statement of great simplicity and power. The

31

Second Law introduces the notion of entropy. Entropy is a measure of how 'spread out' the energy is. The Second Law is merely a statement of fact that, in all known processes, the overall entropy never diminishes, and usually it increases so that the universe becomes more disordered. It also leads to an important distinction between two types of energy transfers, those that happen spontaneously and those that happen deliberately.

Differences in temperatures between objects lead to the spontaneous redistribution of energy such that the system reaches an equilibrium. Because there are more ways of spreading the energy around over many objects than localising it in a few, the energy goes from the concentrated localised form (the small hot object) to warm the surrounding objects and spreads out (the entropy increases). Such spontaneous events always result in energy spreading out. This limits the possibilities of what is physically achievable. Fuels (and oxygen) are concentrated stores of energy which, when burnt, spontaneously transfer energy. These stores of concentrated energy are limited, hence the necessity to 'Save it' where the 'it' is fuel and not energy. After burning the fuel there is

2.1 Campaign slogan issued by Department of Energy

exactly the same amount of energy as there was before but it is not localised. It has become spread out and is less useful to us as it is very difficult to collect the energy together again. The chances of it spontaneously collecting together again are so remote that it is a virtual impossibility.

Deliberate events are done by transferring energy through work and do not happen spontaneously. Energy is accumulated in one store at the expense of spreading a lot of energy around elsewhere. A power station has to spread a lot of energy over many millions of molecules in the air in order to concentrate a limited amount of energy on electrical charges. Concentrating energy in one place can only be done at the expense of spreading a lot of energy around elsewhere so the best power stations are only 30–40% efficient. Similarly, a human being has to dissipate a lot of energy heating their surroundings in order to transfer a limited amount of energy to a few bags by lifting them higher. The basic reason for this is that deliberate transfers of energy concentrate energy on a few objects such as a book on a shelf. The result is that the Universe is more ordered as energy has been stored on a limited number of objects as potential energy between the book and the Earth. This happens spontaneously so rarely in nature that it is just never seen. How many books are observed to pick themselves up off the floor? So energy can only be concentrated on a few objects by spreading a lot of energy around elsewhere. This is why power stations need large cooling towers: 30–40% of their energy is concentrated on electrical charges but only at the expense of transferring a lot of energy to the atmosphere via the cooling towers.

Deliberate transfers of energy are what the physicist measures through the classical definition of work done = force × distance or electrical energy transferred = voltage × current × time.

There is another notion prevalent here, the idea that energy transferred by heating is 'degraded'. This is not true. To use the money analogy, it is as if the money has been devalued. Energy is energy, just as money is money. It is just that the result of transferring energy by heating is to spread the energy around many millions of objects rather like some millionaire sharing their wealth with the poor. There is still the same amount of money at the end, it is just that it is not concentrated in one location.

Implications for Science Education

The preceding discussion implies that the long-term goals of an education in science about energy should be to
  (a) develop an understanding that energy is conserved and that in any process the total energy is the same before as after;
  (b) left to itself, energy spontaneously spreads out and becomes less usable. Energy moves from hot to cold objects spontaneously.
It implies that in any treatment of energy, the following should apply:
  (a) It is acceptable to talk of cornflakes, fuels and sunshine having energy but that should be extended to make children aware that the energy is associated with the combination of fuel and oxygen.
  (b) With the exception of kinetic and potential energy, the notion of forms of energy should not be used apart from in a very informal sense. It is much more useful to talk about *transferring* energy rather than transforming it.
  (c) Energy should not be introduced as the causal factor in any process. Energy is not necessary to make things go. Energy exists and its origins lie in the early history of the Universe. Objects are not dependent on a supply of energy to make them go. For instance the Moon and the Earth keep going quite happily without a supply of energy! A lack of energy limits what is possible though. Hence it would be better to say that energy is needed to lift things or to change things.

(d) Children need to have much more experience of the idea that energy 'spreads out' and is dissipated. This does not mean that they should be given a formal introduction to the idea of entropy!

When energy 'spreads out', it becomes less 'useful' energy. The principal mechanism for 'spreading' energy is friction which acts between surfaces. Only if children have a prior understanding of friction as a force between surfaces can they see that doing work against this force transfers energy by heating the surrounds. A marble rolling on a friction-free, horizontal glass plate does not need any work to be done to maintain its motion at constant velocity, and energy is not transferred elsewhere (figure 2.2). Of course, any real marble

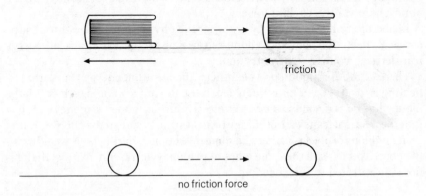

friction

no friction force

2.2 Two situations where work is required and where no work is needed

moving on any real horizontal surface will slow down as there is friction between the surfaces, and this force acting on the marble transfers energy by heating the surface of the plate. The result is that the concentrated energy of the marble is 'spread out' over many millions of molecules.

Talking about energy in the classroom

The following is an attempt to define some useful ways of talking about energy in the classroom. For children, a set of simple operational descriptions is more useful than any attempt at an elementary definition. The physicist's notion of work done is not particularly helpful and it applies only to deliberate energy transfers and is quantitative rather than qualitative. Children should have an opportunity to be introduced to energy as an important idea whilst in the lower secondary school. Such an introduction should try to place an emphasis on the notion of energy as a universal currency which is transferred from one location to another. For example, a battery transfers energy stored in the chemicals to the electrical charges which transfer it to the light emitted from the battery. This means that the traditional term for the apparatus commonly used in schools is a misnomer. They are *not* energy conversion kits but *energy transfer* kits! All the observed effects can be explained in terms of transferring energy by working or by heating.

In all these discussions it is helpful to place an emphasis on the idea that energy 'spreads out' more than on the idea that energy is conserved. Solomon[4] suggests that the former is more natural and intuitive for children. It is only after children begin to understand that transfers of energy often result in energy going to many objects that they can begin to appreciate that the total sum of energy may be conserved, even if the available or 'useful' energy is diminished as a result of this process. Conservation of energy should only be treated implicitly and no attempt made to justify it. After all, there is no classroom evidence available to justify it. Most classroom experiments fail to show that energy is conserved as it is impossible to do all the accounting accurately. The justification in most physics courses relies on a historical treatment which depends on children believing in the validity of historical evidence.

So any treatment should start from the notion that fuels, including food, have a commodity called energy. Whenever any change occurs energy is transferred from one object to another and without a supply of energy it is impossible to do certain processes. As a result energy is *needed to make deliberate changes occur*.

- ○ Energy is needed *to lift things*.
- ○ Energy is needed *to make things hotter*.
- ○ Energy is needed *to make things move faster*.
- ○ Energy is needed *to change the shape of things*.

This form of talking about energy does not imply that the energy 'makes things go'. Pushes and pulls are what change objects' motion and position and pushes and pulls are a means of transferring energy. Energy merely limits the process. Energy is needed to raise objects and without a source of energy it is impossible to lift them. Without a supply of energy it is impossible to exert a force and alter the velocity of an object.

- ○ Energy can be *stored*
- ○ Energy can be *stored in springs*.
- ○ Energy can be *stored in vibrating or moving molecules*.
- ○ Energy can be *stored in an atomic nuclei*.
- ○ Energy can be *stored by lifting masses in a gravitational field*.

Moving objects have *kinetic energy* and energy can be transferred from one location to another. It is best not to think of the different forms of energy as physically different things ('The kinetic energy turned to potential energy.'), but as the same energy taking on different disguises ('The energy of the car was transferred from kinetic to potential as it went uphill.').

Fuels and oxygen must be viewed as concentrated stores of energy. Such energy can be released spontaneously by combustion to do useful work such as move a car. However, a large percentage of the energy has to be spread out heating the atmosphere (90% in a car) in order to concentrate a limited amount of energy in the form of kinetic energy of the car.

Consider the energy flows in a model steam engine (figure 2.3). Energy in the fuel and oxygen heats the air, which by a process of convection and conduction heats the water inside the boiler. The extra energy is sufficient to cause some of

35

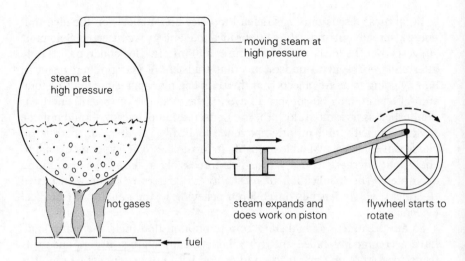

steam at
high pressure

moving steam at
high pressure

hot gases

steam expands and
does work on piston

flywheel starts to
rotate

fuel

(necessary valves omitted for clarity)

2.3 Model steam engine

the water to boil into steam at high pressure. The steam passes down a tube, causing a net flow of energy along the tube. Part of the energy is kinetic and part is the potential energy of the pressurised steam. The steam eventually does work by expanding against a piston, which transmits the energy to the kinetic energy of the flywheel. The energy is than transmitted along a shaft, or by a belt, to a generator which transfers the energy to the electrical charges in the wire.

Both of these examples show that energy is merely being used as some kind of interconvertible currency which takes on many different disguises but is essentially the same thing. Both show how it is possible to avoid talking about 'forms' of energy.

There are several problems associated with energy transfers, some of which have already been discussed. There are, however, a few more which require closer examination.

The 'conservation of energy'/'Save it!' paradox

This paradox illustrates many of the confusions about energy. If energy is conserved, why do we need to save it? The answer lies in the fact that there has been a confusion between energy and fuel. Fuels (and oxygen) are concentrated sources of energy which can be released spontaneously by burning. Some of this energy can be deliberately diverted to perform useful processes. However, much of this energy is dissipated. Dissipation is the 'spreading out' of 'heat' energy, making it more dilute, and hence reducing its temperature. Ogborn[5] introduces the idea of 'available energy', that is energy available for use. Both of these approaches can be useful and are used in the examples below.

When energy is transformed from electrical charges to light in a tungsten filament light bulb, only 2% of the input electrical energy is transformed to

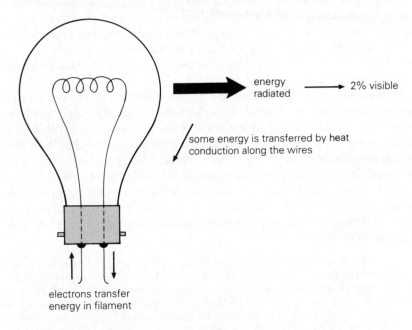

2.4 Transfer of energy in a tungsten filament light bulb

light. The other 98% goes to heat the local environment. A fluorescent light is much more efficient than a tungsten light bulb, but still only converts or transfers less than half of the input energy to light energy. During the process most of the energy has been transferred by heating to the local surroundings and the filament; the result is that the energy has been 'spread out' and is less useful. Most of the energy has become 'less available' to do useful work.

A millionaire could do useful things with his or her money, such as build some homes for the poor or open a new hospital. If instead he or she chooses to drop the money out of the window on the top floor of a skyscraper, the money is spread out amongst many thousands of people who cannot do anything particularly useful with it. What is more, once distributed, it is practically impossible to collect it all together again.

When energy 'runs down' or becomes less available, it is usually because it is dissipated into a large mass. 'Waste' energy is usually at too low a temperature to be useful. At the Atomic Energy Research Establishment at Harwell there is an experimental nuclear reactor (PLUTO) that produces what would, at first sight, seem to be a useful 10 MW of energy. If it could be sufficiently concentrated, this amount of energy would be enough to supply 10 000 electric fires. Unfortunately, the energy is not very 'available'; it is highly dissipated, and is carried by large amounts of water at only 80 °C. This is not hot enough to run steam turbines and is just used to heat the local air! In some power stations this energy is now used to heat greenhouses and produce tomatoes for retail.

37

Another example is that of a burning match being used to heat a bath full of cold water. Assuming that all the 'available energy' transferred by the combustion of the wood of the match heats the water in the bath, the temperature of the water increases by a small fraction of a degree, whereas the temperature of the flame was around 1000 °C. The energy transformed by the burning match has been dissipated, spread out, and in doing so become much less useful. The energy has become less available to do useful things but the total quantity remains the same.

Permeating all of this discussion in class is the physicist's belief in the conservation of energy. The law of conservation of energy is one which has never been violated so far as we know. Indeed, if an experiment were to demonstrate violation, the immediate explanation would be that the energy was being converted to a form which the experimental apparatus did not measure. Unfortunately it is a practical impossibility for any teacher of physics to demonstrate it to their class. This is simply because in any energy transfer process it is very difficult to account for all the energy unless extreme care is taken to measure all the energy transfers taking place. Feynman[6] gives an apt illustration of this.

> 'Imagine Denise, who has some building blocks which are absolutely indestructible and cannot be divided into pieces. Let us suppose she has 28 blocks. Each is the same as the other. Her father puts her with the 28 blocks into a room at the beginning of the day. At the end of the day, being curious, he counts the blocks very carefully and discovers a phenomenal law – no matter what Denise does with the blocks there are always 28 remaining! This continues for a number of days, until one day there are only 27 blocks, but a little investigation shows that there is one under the rug. One day, however, the number appears to change – there are only 26 blocks. Careful investigation indicates that the window was open, and upon looking outside, the two other blocks are found. Another day a careful count indicates that there are 30 blocks. This causes considerable consternation until it is realised that Bruce came to visit bringing blocks with him. . .'

For our pupils, the law of conservation of energy is inevitably an act of faith based on an historical exposition of the experiments performed by Count Rumford and Joule. However, presented in a lively and illustrated fashion, it makes an entertaining tale of human endeavour.[7] Alternatively this is an ideal opportunity for pupils to use resources to do some project work on the historical development of an important idea.

'Heat' energy and internal energy

'Heat' is not a substance or a property but a process. When something is heated (or cooled), energy is transferred from one place to another so as to cause a change in temperature. Heating or cooling an object alters its internal energy. The internal energy in the system at any instant is the sum of the kinetic energy of all the atoms and the potential energy stored in all the bonds. It is not a 'form of energy' but a way of describing the fact that the energy in atoms is both stored and kinetic energy.

The simplest visualisation of a solid is an array of particles joined by spring-like bonds. Many science departments have a model like this for sodium chloride crystals. At any temperature above absolute zero the particles are oscillating randomly. The kinetic energy of any individual atom or bond is constantly changing, but the total internal energy in the solid is constant at a particular temperature. Internal energy is sometimes referred to as thermal energy. If a car collides with a tree, some of the kinetic energy is transferred to internal energy and raises the temperature of the car and the tree, and some to other forms of energy such as sound. However, this description can only be used with children who have been introduced to a microscopic view of matter.

Before this, with some thought, it is possible to avoid the use of the word 'heat' as a noun entirely, and to use it exclusively as a verb unless using it colloquially, such as 'the heat of the fire is very fierce'. If the emphasis is placed on the *transfer*, teachers can talk simply about the energy being transferred by heating from one object to another. If this is too difficult, the best compromise, certainly up to GCSE level, is to refer to either internal or thermal energy consistently. Internal energy is not a form of energy but merely a way of distinguishing that the energy associated with the atoms of an object is both potential and kinetic energy which are constantly being interchanged. Unfortunately many textbooks and syllabuses still use 'heat' as a noun. However, *Nuffield 13–16*, and *Nuffield Co-ordinated Sciences* are both good examples of texts that manage to avoid this pitfall.

Here are two illustrations and a brief discussion of each.

'The boiler is heating the house.'

The energy that is released by burning a fuel in the boiler is transferred to the water by heating. This is then transferred to the air near the radiators by conduction and convection. This increased (internal) energy is then dissipated through the house, and eventually is transferred from the house to the air outside, increasing its (internal) energy. If the insulation of the house were made more efficient, the house would transfer (internal) energy more slowly, and the boiler would need to operate less frequently to maintain the desired temperature.

'I'm warming this piece of ice to melt it.'

'Warming' here is a synonym of 'heating'. Although the temperature of the ice is not increasing, the internal energy is increasing as the ice melts. Energy must be supplied to do the work needed to separate the H_2O molecules against the forces holding them together. This is the 'latent heat of fusion', so-called because the increase in (internal) energy during melting is hidden and not accompanied by any corresponding temperature change.

Ultimately, careful and precise use of the words 'heat' and 'energy' will help pupils to refine their own understanding of these ideas.

Finally, one of the phenomena that puzzles pupils is why someone holding an object should get tired. After all, there is no movement and no apparent transfer of energy, so why does anybody need a supply of energy to do this? While it is true that a shelf is able to support a 1 kg bag of sugar indefinitely without any energy input, it is everyday experience that the same is not true for people. It is almost as tiring to support a weight as it is to lift it. This is due to the nature of muscles. A muscle consists of a large number of individual muscle cells each of which can either be contracted or not. The contraction is caused by a neurochemical process which cannot be sustained for a long period. A prolonged effort is characterised by the continuous contracting and relaxing of muscle cells (figure. 2.5). What seems to be a steady push is the averaged-out

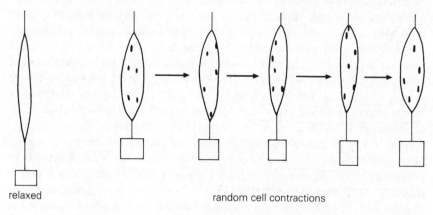

relaxed   random cell contractions

2.5 Method by which muscle maintains prolonged contraction

effect of these multiple contractions and relaxations. There is no energy transfer to the object held, but energy is dissipated by heating the muscles as they do work contracting and expanding causing the physical sensation of tiredness.

Teaching energy

When starting the teaching of energy, teachers will find it interesting to see the responses they obtain when they ask children to write four different sentences containing the word 'energy'. Another approach is to ask children to work in groups and produce a poster illustrating what is meant by the word 'energy.' This encourages children to verbalise their ideas. It is not a sensible teaching strategy to ignore the learners' existing conceptual framework and to provide a different and unnatural framework of scientific ideas that will wither for lack of roots. One coherent approach to the teaching of energy is provided by the Children's Learning in Science Project which has produced a resource pack, *Approaches to Teaching Energy*.[8] This pack provides useful helpful examples of pupils' work, guidance for successfully developing small group work, reporting back and other methods. The basic approach is to 'start from where the pupils are', to elicit their ideas and then help pupils to restructure them into a form which is closer to the scientific view.

Teachers may think that this extensive and time-consuming teaching and learning process is unnecessary. However, there is substantial evidence from the Assessment of Performance Unit[9] that traditional approaches fail to produce the required understanding in children. It is instructive to study the results obtained by the CLIS project[10] in their study on secondary students' understanding of 'heat' energy as an example. In the items used by this team with 15-year-old students:

○ only 5% gave complete responses based on accepted ideas about change of state;

○ less than 20% gave complete arguments based on accepted ideas of conduction;

○ almost 70% gave partially complete explanations based on 'heat' transfer towards a body, less than 20% gave similar explanations based on 'heat' transfer away from a body.

Most introductory approaches to the teaching of energy concentrate on posing the following questions.

○ Where does energy come from?

○ What happens to the energy when it is transferred?

○ What are the different forms of energy?

It has been argued here that discussion of forms of energy is not a useful approach. Very often, energy is introduced to children as a topic in the 11–14 age range and the normal approach is to make use of an 'energy circus' which consists of a plethora of small experiments designed to demonstrate the 'conversion' of energy from 'one form to another'. However, this can be avoided by concentrating on the transfer of energy and calling it an 'energy transfer' kit. Children will see energy as some kind of commodity which is transferred from one location to another in these experiments. This is more useful than any notion of 'light energy', 'sound energy' or other 'forms of energy'.

These experiments are also fairly convincing demonstrations that energy appears to 'run out'. For the teacher this has to be the starting point. Yes, the energy does appear to 'run out' but has it gone forever? Introduce the idea that some people think the energy has been transferred to locations that have not been accounted for. Pupils should be sent back to the experiments to see if they can observe where the energy might possibly have gone. Has the object got warmer? Was there any light emitted or sound produced? All of these require energy. This sows the seeds of doubt about whether the energy does disappear and helps to introduce the idea that 'all the energy is conserved'. Pupils should be encouraged to use Sankey diagrams to show the energy flows rather than the normal simplistic box diagrams. Here the width of the arrow shows what proportion of the original energy is transferred to different locations. In figure 2.6, it shows that the majority of the energy is transferred by heating to the atmosphere and a tiny fraction is transferred away by light. There is no expectation that they should get the right proportions, but the diagrams are an effective reminder that in most energy transfers the energy is transferred in a variety of ways. Adding up all these transfers leaves the same number at the end as at the beginning. Much of this work is aimed at developing a good tacit understanding of a concept which will be covered again in the fourth year.

The programme of study for GCSE introduces children to the idea that energy can be measured when it is transferred. What is being measured is the amount of energy deliberately transferred by a force acting through a distance and there is an intuitive argument to justify the idea. Essentially pushing (or pulling)

41

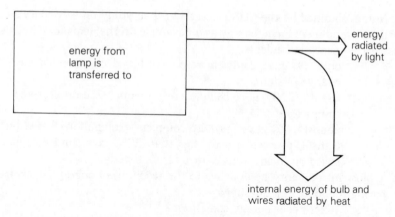

energy
radiated
by light

energy from
lamp is
transferred to

internal energy of bulb and
wires radiated by heat

2.6 Sankey diagram for energy transfer in a light bulb

twice as hard requires twice as much energy. Pushing (or pulling) for twice the distance requires twice as much energy. Pushing, or pulling, with twice as much force over twice as much distance requires four times as much energy. The idea of a definition of energy transfer which encompasses these ideas can then be introduced.

Work done = energy transferred = force × distance

This definition introduces the idea of a joule of energy. However, this should not be an unfamiliar unit as children commonly meet it in 11–14 work in analysing the nutritional value of food.

The standard treatment then uses a selection of experiments with pulleys, jacks, levers and other energy transfer devices to develop confidence and familiarity with the measurement of energy and introduce the notion of efficiency. Efficiency is a measure of how successful we are at transferring the energy deliberately the way we want to transfer it. If the idea that energy 'spreads out' has been introduced and pupils are familiar with friction as a mechanism which transfers energy in unwanted ways, they should appreciate that it is difficult to produce a machine which is 100% efficient. Pupils should have the opportunity to measure the efficiencies of a range of devices.

Following on from efficiency, most courses move to introducing the idea of power.

Power is generally associated by children with strength. A stronger individual is more powerful because they can exert larger forces. While this is true, children need to be introduced to the idea that in scientific terms, power measures how fast the energy is transferred. A motor is more powerful than another if it lifts a weight faster. There is an exciting experiment here where they can measure their own power by calculating how fast they transfer energy from their muscles to stored energy when they run up stairs. It is not necessarily the fastest person who is the most powerful.

Most courses will also introduce the methods of measuring the energy transfer in heating an object. Again this is a deliberate transfer of energy and it is best approached experimentally by showing that the same amount of energy supplied to different substances does not raise the temperature by the same amount. This observation is the basis for arguing for the idea of the 'specific heat capacity' of a substance which is the amount of energy needed to raise 1 kg by 1 °Celsius. This quantity can then be used to calculate the amount of energy transferred by heating by arguing that a 2 °C rise requires twice as much energy. If the object is twice as massive, it will require twice as much energy for a 1 °C rise in temperature. Heating a 2 kg mass through a 2 °C temperature rise requires four times as much energy. This intuitive approach is much more satisfactory than producing the standard formula and expecting children to memorise it.

Finally energy reappears in the study of electricity. It is important that children understand that electricity is merely a method of transferring energy from one location to another. In a simple circuit, the battery transfers energy to the electric charges which transfer it to the filament by heating and this energy is radiated by the lamp. The electricity meter measures the amount of energy transferred and not the amount of electricity 'used'. The current in the circuit is conserved so the electric charges are not used up.

If children have already met the idea of power and its measurement in watts, it is simpler to approach the measurement of electrical energy by investigations of the markings on electrical appliances, tabulating the appliance and its power. This can then lead to an introduction of the non-standard unit of energy transferred, the kilowatt-hour and pupils can calculate the cost of running a variety of electrical appliances.

Further discussion of energy is found in the references. The approach varies from a purist approach, for example that of Warren[11], to a pragmatic approach in which it is accepted that children use the words and hold a life-world meaning for them without teacher intervention[4]. Warren sees energy as being a concept that is too difficult a topic even to be mentioned in elementary courses. However such a view would deny an opportunity to most pupils to develop a better understanding of the topic. Energy is now even seen as a valid concept to study 'across the curriculum' particularly in the humanities[12]. Science teachers should use this opportunity to work with colleagues so that children can develop a coherent and consistent understanding. The future citizen equipped with a better understanding of energy and science is hopefully more likely to make a more informed choice about energy sources and to use it in a more socially responsible manner.

Notes and references

1 The unit *Energy* and the associated *Energy: A Teachers' Guide*, *Nuffield Science 13–16*, (1979) Longmans, take this view of energy and articulate an exemplary approach to the teaching of energy.

2 Adams B. (1988) 'Energy: transfer or conversion?' *School Science Review*, **69**, 603.

3 This means that a moving object is tangibly more massive than the object at rest so we can 'feel the energy' if we attempt to kick it. The increase in mass is practically negligible but it does mean that energy is a real quantity. There is a common misconception in many popular texts that mass and energy are

convertible from one form to another. This is not so. Energy behaves as if it had mass but mass cannot be converted to energy. For a fuller discussion of this see the article by Bondi H. & Spurgin C.B. (1987) 'Energy has mass'. *Physics Bulletin*, **38**, 2, pp. 62–3.

4 Solomon J. (1982) 'How children learn about energy, or, Does the first law come first?', *School Science Review*, **63**, **224**, 415–22.
5 Ogborn J. (1982) 'Energy and fuel: The meaning of the 'go of things', *School Science Review*, **68**, **242**, 30–5.
6 Feynman R. (1963) *The Feynman Lectures of Physics*, vol. 1, 4–1. Addison-Wesley, Massachusetts.
7 For a fairly thorough treatment of this see *Revised Nuffield Physics, Teachers Guide Year* (1978) pp. 171–80, Longmans.
8 *Approach to Teaching Energy* (1988): Part of a pack of materials produced by the Children's Learning in Science Project, Centre for Studies in Science and Mathematics Education, Leeds University, Leeds LS2 9JT.
9 For a typical example see *Science at Age 15* (1985): Assessment of Performance Unit. Department of Education and Science.
10 Brook A., Briggs H., Bell B. & Driver R. (1984) *'The Children's Learning in Science Project (CLIS): Aspects of secondary students' understanding of 'heat'*, University of Leeds.
11 Warren J.W. (1982) 'The nature of energy', *European Journal of Science Education*, **4**, no. 3, 295–7.
12 Scott J. (1986) *'Energy through time.'* Schools History Project 13–16. Oxford University Press.

3 Electricity and magnetism

Electricity

Unfortunately for the teacher electricity is invisible and only its effects can be observed. This makes the ideas abstract, and it is only through extended observation, experiment and discussion that students can develop an understanding. It is a considerable surprise to many physics teachers when they review the research results from the Assessment of Performance Unit (APU) and others for the first time. For instance, Shipstone[1] quotes research findings that indicate that only 50% of students at 16 were able to predict the effect of adding further bulbs in series to an existing circuit. Various researchers (see for example Shipstone[1], Osborne & Freyberg[2], and the APU[3]) have found that a large fraction of students at age 15 use one or several 'alternative' working models, some of which account for some observed features of circuits but are mutually inconsistent. Indeed some pupils seem to change their model depending on the problem they are solving. The most common alternative models seem to be the following.

(a) *The 'clashing currents' model.* Current leaves the battery at both terminals (figure 3.1). Pupils may think explicity of two types of electricity. The reaction of the currents in the bulb causes the light.
(b) *Dilution of current.* Current becomes weaker round the circuit (figure 3.2). The return wire may not be necessary. The current is shared so that, in a three-bulb circuit, each bulb takes one third of the current. This accounts for their relative dimness when compared with a single-bulb circuit.
(c) *Single wire.* The second wire is not necessary (figure 3.3). There will be no current in it as the electricity is converted to light in the bulb.

It is clear that pupils have deeply ingrained ideas about the nature of electricity that they bring with them to science lessons[4]. They attempt to use these perceptions about the way the world works to make sense of their observations in science. It is when the observations they make are in conflict with their model, and when pupils are encouraged to question their model, extending or modifying it as necessary, that learning takes place.

It is worth spending some time on the crucial ideas of circuits, and in particular the constancy of the current round a series circuit. This fundamental idea is often insufficiently emphasised in many courses. It also leads to an immediate paradox for many students: if the current leaving a battery is the same as that entering it, why does the battery ever run down? Unless pupils comprehend the ideas behind circuits, they will be unable safely or efficiently to solve electrical problems in the home, in cars, or at work.

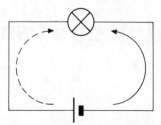

3.1 Clashing currents model of flow of electricity in a circuit

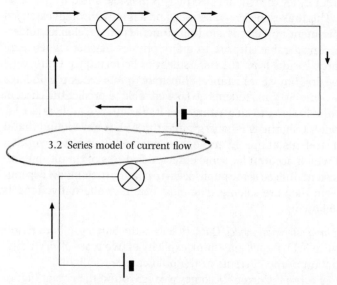

3.2 Series model of current flow

3.3 Single wire model of current flow

Two types of strategy are directly relevant to these difficulties. First, pupils must be allowed to experiment in an open-ended way with circuit components. Practical problems must be set, and pupils must find an answer for themselves, with minimal guidance. Secondly, visible analogies for electricity can be demonstrated.

For example, a simple task might be set of making a bulb light using a battery, a bulb, and several wires. This task has been used in research by Osborne & Freyberg with a group of 40 pupils aged between 8 and 12. 33 of the children initially failed, of whom six eventually succeeded. This task introduced to the children the idea that the circuit must be complete and that an ordinary bulb has two terminals. It is also very good for revealing children's alternative conceptions about current flow. A similar activity, perhaps at a slightly higher level of sophistication, that could be used with pupils older than this is to show pupils a simple series circuit and ask them to discuss in groups what size current measurements they would obtain before and after the bulb with an ammeter. They can then be asked to perform the experiment and discuss whether their predictions were correct. This will cause a conflict for children operating with a 'series' model of electricity who see it as being 'used up' in circuit components.

An increasing number of children will have used batteries and bulbs in primary school science; this will typically have been solving simple problems with little if any theoretical background, although the idea of a circuit will probably have been introduced.

Science in Process[5], the ILEA materials for 11–13 science, include a problem-solving activity based on a simple torch. This activity also suggests that pupils should observe a torch bulb with a hand lens, account for the features seen, and infer the route of the connecting wires. One of the authors[6] has proposed a simple set of problems based on car electrical systems. These problems require an extension of the logic of simple circuits to circuits with a common, uninsulated return conductor. A novel approach to the teaching of electrical concepts that is based on applications in the home is taken by Nuffield Home Economics[7]. This approach makes use of an extensive range of home appliances to introduce concepts of electricity as a means of supplying energy, electric current and power and would be well suited to those who may be less motivated by the conventional approach as the science is introduced in a context that has personal meaning.

The second type of strategy is based on making the current in a circuit visible, by using a concrete model for a circuit. It is helpful to refer back to any model frequently, to point out defects as well as similarities, and to ask pupils to use the model themselves to simulate their own circuits, as an aid to problem solving.

Useful models of electric circuits, currents and voltages

One model which is very useful, even though it has limitations, is the water circuit (figure 3.4). In this model, the rate of flow of water is analogous to the electric current, which is a measure of the rate of flow of electrons, and is the

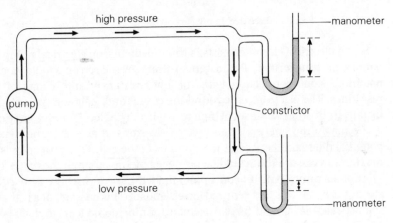

high pressure

manometer

pump

constrictor

low pressure

manometer

3.4 Water circuit model

same all the way round a circuit with no junctions (a series circuit). The water (current) is not used up, and the function of the return tube (wire) in the circuit is easily explained. Cosgrove & Osborne[8] found that experiments to establish the equality of water flow (current) round simple series circuits are crucial in helping students to establish the concept of a circuit. The pump in the circuit is analogous to the battery, supplying energy to the water which is dissipated through friction in the circuit. A constriction in the water circuit is analogous to resistance in an electrical circuit. The connecting pipes and wires are assumed to have no significant resistance in either the water or electrical circuits.

The hydrostatic pressure, as measured by a manometer, at any point in the water circuit is analogous to the electrical potential at that point in the circuit. The more familiar concept of potential difference is measured by a manometer connected between two points on the water circuit. The pump raises the water to a higher pressure (gives the water a higher potential). The water flows round the circuit unimpeded until it reaches the constriction, in which the pressure falls (there is a potential drop). There can be a potential difference between two places even though no current is flowing (figure 3.5); this is the normal condition between the two terminals of a disconnected battery. The equivalent for a water circuit is a dam with water stored up behind it.

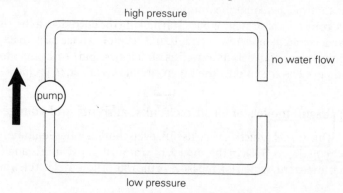

3.5 'Potential difference' in a water circuit

So, an electrical circuit consists of three elements: an electrical pump (a cell, battery or transformer, for instance) that gives electrons some energy or potential, some connecting wires of low resistance, and a load of higher resistance. The electrons flow round the circuit and their energy is dissipated, usually by heating, at places of high resistance. The electromotive force of a cell is the maximum energy it can give to electrons, that is it is the maximum potential difference between the terminals of the cell. This corresponds to the maximum pressure that could be produced by the pump in the water circuit.

Another rather fanciful conceptual model that can usefully be used for an electric circuit is the 'couriers and jewels' model. This operates at a rather more sophisticated level, and has an element of mnemonic learning! The courier (coulombs of charge) move round a circuit between a factory (cell) and a shop (bulb) carrying jewels (joules of energy) where they are sold (figure 3.6). The rate of passage of couriers (current) is going to be, on average, the same whenever it is measured round the circuit. Each courier can carry a variable number of jewels from the factory to the shop, and returns empty-handed to the factory. This corresponds to the fact that each electron in a circuit can have

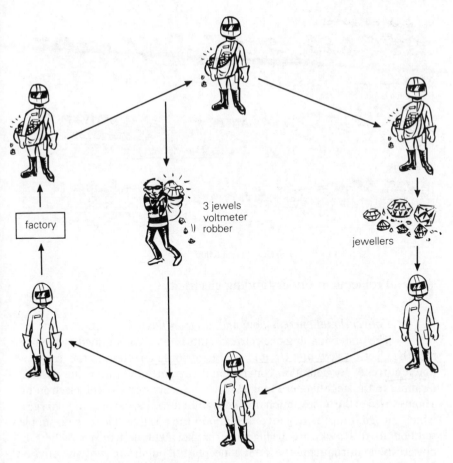

3.6 'Coulombs' and 'Joules' model of a circuit

varying amounts of energy. Occasionally a robber (voltmeter) diverts a courier from the shop, steals and counts his jewels, and returns the courier to the factory.

Another model that can be used with some effect is the 'central heating' model. Central heating systems depend on a flow of water round a circuit, heated by a boiler and transferring energy at radiators. The current is the rate of flow of water, and the boiler and pump correspond to the battery which supply energy to the water. The energy is transported to the radiators where it is transferred to internal energy of the air. However, as with all models it should be used with care and its limitations recognised. The radiator is not a constriction in the circuit but a very large pipe which offers low resistance to the passage of water through itself.

Finally a simpler anthropomorphic model is provided by Peter Warren in the delightful cartoons he uses in his book *Investigating Electricity*[9]. Not only are these clear and amusing, but they provide concrete visual models of many simple electrical phenomena. In addition, they clearly show that the carriers of charge are not 'used up' as they pass through resistors and bulbs (figure 3.7).

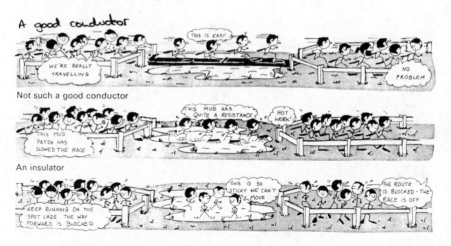

3.7 Cartoon models of electrical conduction

Problems in understanding electricity

Conventional current flow and electron flow

The understanding of electric circuits is often confounded by the fact that the electron flow in a circuit is in the opposite direction to the 'conventional current'. By definition conventional current moves from the positive terminal to the negative terminal. However, the discovery of the electron by Thomson led to the appreciation that it was the electrons, the negative charges, which moved from the negative terminal to the positive. There is no simple solution to this awkward pedagogical predicament and most teachers of physics avoid introducing the latter concept until pupils are studying physics for a GCSE course. The conventional view minimises any difficulties with circuit construction.

There are several computer packages available that allow the construction of circuits and the animation of currents flowing. An example is *Circuits*[10], from the Electricity Council, which allows on-screen construction of a circuit with cells, bulbs, connecting wires and switches. The circuit can then be tested, with the current in different wires being indicated by an animated display. This can then be analysed by the students, and the predictions made from the display confirmed using real circuit components.

Voltage, potential difference and electromotive force (e.m.f.)

One source of confusion in discussing electrical circuits is the use of the terms potential, voltage and e.m.f. Electric potential is a measure of the energy per unit charge. As electrons go round a circuit they lose electric potential. The normal expression is to say that 'the potential drops'. The potential difference across a component is just the difference of potential between the electrons entering and leaving a component. The potential difference (p.d.) is measured in volts, that is, the number of joules for each coulomb of charge, and it is often referred to as the voltage across a component. The potential difference developed across a cell is called the electromotive force, e.m.f., also measured in volts, and also often misnamed voltage. It is better to avoid the term 'voltage' and to use potential difference or electromotive force explicitly.

The height analogy for potential is useful and easy to put across. Simply stated, gravitational potential energy can be used as an analogue for electrical potential energy. In this model, a cell lifts electrons to a height governed by the e.m.f. of the cell, and the electrons fall back downhill and give up energy as they pass through resistances on their way back to the cell (figure 3.8).

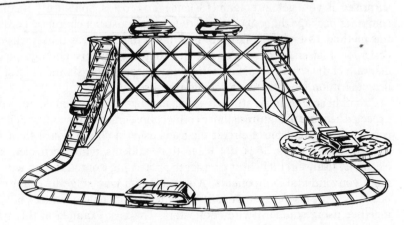

3.8 Gravitational model of a circuit

Resistance and Ohm's Law

Another pedagogic difficulty is introduced with the concept of resistance and Ohm's Law. The term 'law' in science has a wide variety of meanings. In this instance it is a statement of the relationship between the potential difference across a component and the current through it.

> 'With a certain subclass of conductors, and at constant temperature, the current passing through the conductor is proportional to the potential difference across the conductor.'

Ohm's 'Law' applies only to metals, and not to electrolytes, gases or plasmas. It would be better called a 'rule', but the terminology is too well established (as it is with another 'law', 'Hooke's Law'). Another common misinterpretation of this is to say that

$$V = I \times R$$

is a statement of Ohm's Law! This is not true as this expression is the definition of resistance!

Pupils should be shown that resistance does vary with temperature and this property is used in many electronic devices to monitor temperatures and control machinery, for example, a thermostat in a fridge.

Practical electricity

Students often experience difficulty in practically constructing simple circuits. One effective guide for students is for them to consider the circuit

51

diagram as a map. This should be taught explicitly. First, the components should be laid out on the bench in the same pattern, and the same way up, as in the diagram. Then the components should be connected together around the circuit, following the circuit with a finger and crossing off each of the sections as the connections are made. Subsidiary (parallel) circuits should be left to the end. The point may usefully be made that if you don't use a map, you must expect to get lost! And if you use a map and hold it upside down, don't be surprised if you get lost again! Science in Process Software[11] includes a computer package that encourages students to construct circuits according to this method. One of the important findings of the APU was that it was much easier for children to construct a circuit if they were given a photograph or 3D diagram of the circuit. Teachers who cannot provide this should at least leave demonstration circuits out for children to use.

Circuit boards seem an attractive idea; in practice they often do not work as expected because of high-resistance connections, and it is often more difficult to construct circuits from a circuit diagram using a circuit board than using discrete components. It is not clear that students who learn elementary electricity using circuit boards transfer their learning to circuits with wires and more conventional components. A sensible half-way stage to using circuit boards is to use discrete components mounted in convenient holders, but wired together using standard wire connectors. The best example of this type of equipment is the Unilab basic electricity kit (figure 3.9).

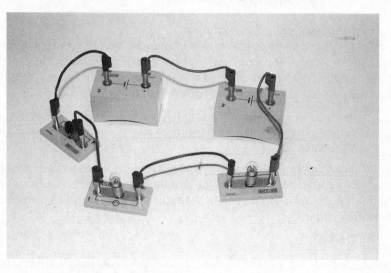

3.9 Unilab basic electricity kit

Another area of much practical difficulty relates to making electrical measurements. The ordinary (and common) two-scale analogue moving-coil meters are the most difficult to make measurements with. The APU[3] have found that only 15% of students at age 15 could read these meters successfully. Fortunately, the introduction of digital meters will alleviate this problem. The student should always be allowed to concentrate on the fundamentals of the science rather than the details of actually reading the meters.

Two specific problems that cause much confusion are bulbs with different ratings and the internal resistance of batteries. The first occurs when two apparently similar bulbs appear to have different brightnesses. The two bulbs should be exchanged and the normal result is that the brighter bulb has moved position. This is due to the fact that the bulbs are not the same and have different resistances and current ratings. This can be checked by looking at the top edge of the metal thread for the specified voltage and current for the bulb. This problem can be avoided by checking the bulbs visually before the lesson.

The second problem occurs when a bulb is added in parallel to an existing bulb; the brightness of the first bulb is reduced. Adding another bulb reduces the brightness of all three yet again. This is because the battery has electrical resistance known as internal resistance. Drawing more current from the battery requires a larger potential difference across the internal resistance. This diminishes the potential difference at the terminals to drive current through the bulbs leading to a consequent reduction in brightness.

Another problem for many students when constructing circuits is that of the third, or earth, wire. They are often aware of the existence of this wire from home experience as a plug clearly has three connections, yet all the circuits they build require only two connections to each component. In mains electrical circuits, the earth wire is a safety device connected to the metal parts of an appliance. If a fault occurs in the appliance so that the frame becomes connected to the live wire, a large current flows in the 'short circuit' between the earth terminal and the live wire. This causes the supply fuse to blow, breaking the connection between the live wire and the appliance making it safe. A good demonstration of this is the 'electric person' which can be found in the Nuffield Home Economics course. Before the fuse is replaced, the cause of the failure must be investigated and put right. The article by Pillner[12], the Understanding Electricity posters[13], or most physics texts provide a more detailed discussion of these problems.

Finally it is important that children understand that electricity is merely a clean and convenient means of transporting energy from one point to another. This is done by transferring energy to electric charge which carries the energy to the load where it is transferred into the required form. The electric charge entering and leaving the device is always the same. The picture with an alternating current is more complex in that the electric charges oscillate as if they were connected in a long chain. The power supply provides the energy to oscillate the chain and this energy is dissipated in the load. Again though, no electric charges are used up!

Magnetism

Most children will have played with magnets at primary school, and may have carried out systematic investigations using them to classify materials. They are fascinated by the action of a magnetic force at a distance. This can be put on a clear observational footing by demonstrations such as two model railway trucks with magnets on a length of railway track (figure 3.10).

Learners can then be stimulated by questions to investigate, such as 'Where is the strongest part of the magnet?' Initial experience leads learners to the

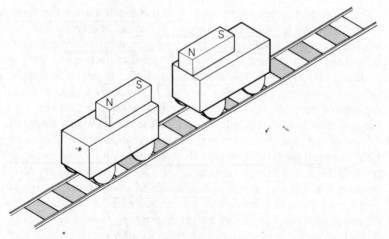

3.10 Simple demonstration of magnetic forces

conclusion that the magnetic effect is concentrated in two parts of the magnet. These 'poles' are often at the ends of the magnet, though this is not universal.

It is worth having a very large magnet for demonstration. This can be used to catch bunches of keys thrown nearby, and is also useful to demonstrate the magnetic effect of an electric current with the arrangement shown in figure 3.11.

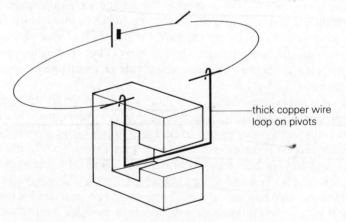

thick copper wire
loop on pivots

3.11 Demonstration of the force on an electric current in a magnetic field

A compass is only a small magnet suspended so that is can turn freely; it lines up with a magnetic field, which comes from one pole of a magnet and goes back to the other pole. Magnetic fields can be plotted using compasses, or can be made visible by using thinly spread 'iron filings'. The best way of doing this is shown in figure 3.12. It is best to tap the paper gently once or twice to help the iron filings line up in the magnetic field.

The temporary pattern can be frozen by photography, or by spraying with an adhesive such as hair lacquer. Driver[14] has pointed out that the diagrams used to show magnetic fields in textbooks are essentially conventional, rather than

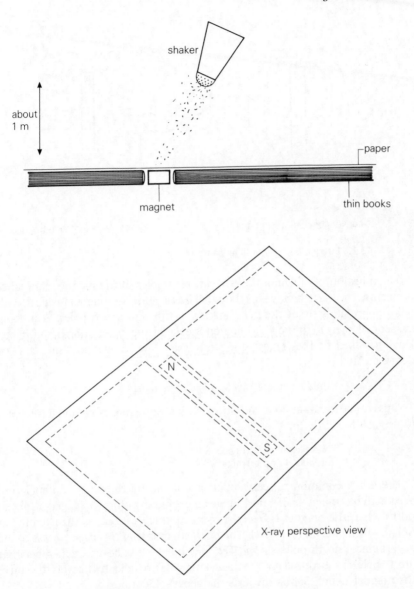

shaker

about 1 m

paper

magnet

thin books

X-ray perspective view

3.12 Plotting a magnetic field with iron filings

accurate representations of what children see. Children when asked to draw the field pattern draw, quite correctly, what they see (figure 3.13). This is not the textbook representation and it is important to spend time on helping learners to abstract a conventional field diagram from a pattern of iron filings.

A useful technique is to carry out the experiment on a sheet of clear plastic over a magnet placed on the stage of an overhead projector. This allows the whole group to discuss the same pattern.

A common misrepresentation of magnetic field patterns is that the poles are on the surface of magnets. Careful observation shows that this is not so; the poles are in fact inside the magnets.

55

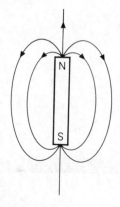

'conventional' representation   typical representation by child

3.13 Interpreting an iron filing pattern

The question of labelling the two different poles of the magnet can cause problems. The Earth behaves as though it has a giant bar magnet inside it, with poles approximately at the geographical north and south poles. A magnet suspended freely in the Earth's magnetic field will line up on a north/south line. Having labelled the poles, the universal law of magnetism can be demonstrated.

'Unlike poles attract and like poles repel.'

This can be learnt as an incantation, with as little meaning, and it is helpful to unpack it a little to:

'N repels N and attracts S,
S repels S and attracts N.'

There is a common misconception about the north/south nomenclature used with bar magnets. If a north pole on a magnet points to the geographical north when the magnet is freely suspended, then it must be attracted by an unlike south pole (figure 3.14). The implication is that *the magnetic pole* at the geographical north pole is a *magnetic south pole*! It is best to remember that 'north pole' is shorthand for 'north-seeking pole' to indicate that it is the end of the magnet which points towards the geographical north.

If a magnet is broken in half, it may be expected that the north and south poles will become separate. In practice this is not so; a new north and south pole are created at the break, and there are two magnets where there was only one before (figure 3.15). It is worth keeping a deliberately broken magnet for this demonstration.

The argument can be continued, and most learners will accept that the ultimate particles making up the magnet must themselves be tiny magnets. Although this is in fact the case, the atoms are grouped together in tiny magnets called 'domains'. In an ordinary piece of iron the domains are randomly aligned; in a magnet the domains are lined up. In steel the domains are more difficult to change direction than in iron, because of the carbon atoms

56

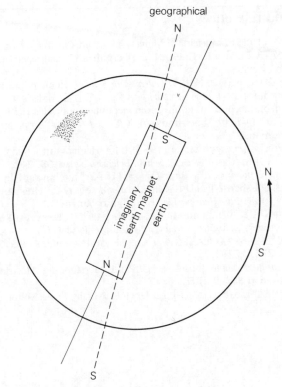

3.14 Poles produced by Earth's magnetic fields

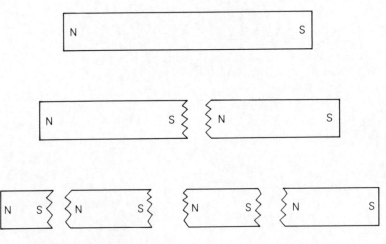

3.15 Effect of breaking a magnet

alloyed with the iron. This makes steel more difficult to magnetise than iron, and more difficult to demagnetise once it has been magnetised.

It is best to store magnets with a 'keeper' that completes the magnetic circuit. This reduces the rate of demagnetisation as the domains vibrate naturally.

Notes and references

1 Shipstone D. (1985) *Electricity in Simple Circuits* in *Children's Ideas and the Learning of Science*, Driver R., Guesne E. & Tiberghien A. (eds.), Open University Press, Milton Keynes.
2 Osborne R. & Freyberg P. (1985) *Learning in Science*. Heinemann, London.
3 APU Science Reports (1984) *Electricity at Age 15*. DES, HMSO.
4 For an amusing account of adult misconceptions about electricity, see the article '*Baffled?*' by Keith Waterhouse in *SCISP Patterns 3, Energy*, pp. 185–6 (1974) Longmans.
5 *Science in Process* (energy theme) (1987) ILEA/Heinemann, London.
6 Freeman J. (1986) 'Car Electrics', *School Science Review*, **68**, **242**, 110.
7 *Nuffield Home Economics: The Basic Course.* (1982) Hutchinson Education.
8 Cosgrove M. & Osborne R. (1985) in *Learning in Science*, Heinemann.
9 Warren P. (1983) *Investigating Electricity*. John Murray.
10 *Circuits* James et al, Longman Microsoftware, Harlow, Essex, (1986).
11 Science in Process Software, *Circuits*, Capital Media (1986).
12 Pillner G.W. (1985) 'On fuses, power supplies and the mains' *School Science Review*, **67**, **238**, 122–4.
13 *Electricity to your home* (posters) (1984) Understanding Electricity, 30 Millbank, London SW1P 4RD.
14 Driver R. (1983) *The Pupil as Scientist?* Open University Press, Milton Keynes.

4 Light

The teaching of light often begins with the concept of rectilinear propagation. Students are introduced to this idea by demonstrations and discussion of why shadows are sharp. Alternatively this idea can be shown directly with a helium–neon laser. Both are useful approaches to the problem, though the laser tends to generate more excitement, expecially if chalk dust is scattered in the beam. However, most physics texts and teachers assume that this concept is so elementary that nearly all children will readily accept it. It is worth noting that this idea was only really evolved by Kepler (1571–1630) in his book *Ad Vitellionen Paralipomena*, and that this took place over several years. Kepler was also the first person to advance a comprehensive theory of vision. He showed that a narrow cone of light rays which went out from a point on an object would be refracted to another point on the retina by the lens and the cornea. It is remarkable how the difficulties or our forebears become the commonplaces of scientific understanding today. It is not surprising then if children have some difficulty with these ideas.

Edith Guesne[1] has shown that children's understanding of light is often limited and inconsistent. Some of the ideas commonly held by children are as follows:

(a) Equating light with its source: some children will commonly perceive light as being resident on the source, that is it is in the bulbs or on the candle.
(b) Light is a state of being: daylight is seen as a result of existing within a sea of light.
(c) Shadows are sometimes seen as reflections of dark light: there is no understanding of the propagation of light and no attempts are made to explain the similarity of shape.
(d) Light 'runs out': a candle fails to light the corners of a room because the source is weak and the light runs out before it gets to the corners. This is obviously linked to children's perceptions. The light cannot be seen hence it has stopped.
(e) Magnifying glasses are seen as making the light bigger so that there is more light behind the glass than in front of it.

These of course contradict the accepted scientific view that light propagates through space in straight lines indefinitely until it is reflected, refracted, scattered or absorbed, and that the common representation is a 'ray' of light.

The situation is no simpler when the behaviour of light in its interaction with matter is considered. Although most children recognise that mirrors reflect light, light incident on ordinary objects is not scattered or reflected but merely stays on the surface. The image seen in a mirror is resident on the surface and

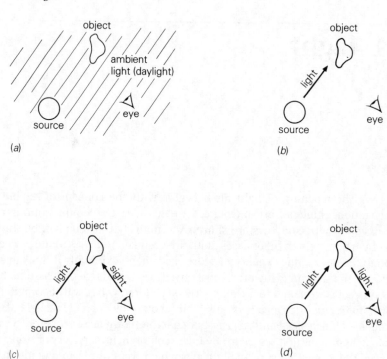

4.1 Common children's view of vision as 'active'

not equidistant behind. Finally vision is not explained in terms of light entering the eye from the object. Figure 4.1 shows how a substantial number of children view the process of vision. This range of ideas about vision have been found to be commonly held by a sample of 13–14 year olds. It reflects the fact that pupils perceive light as being necessary for vision (a) and possibly progress from this to vision as an active process (b and c) to the scientific explanation of vision (d).

That this is so can hardly be surprising when everyday language is full of metaphors which reinforce this notion. A person 'looks daggers' at someone; they cast a 'piercing glance' or their eyes 'sparkle'. The Pythagoreans believed that vision was the result of an invisible fire emanating from the eye and a significant proportion[2,3] of children hold this view.

Given our present knowledge, the introduction to the teaching of light demands a more thorough treatment than that offered in any standard physics text. It is recommended that children are given an opportunity to articulate their own understanding. The Leicestershire group of SSCR[4] have a novel approach in giving children a worksheet of a room with a clock (figure 4.2). The pupils are asked to spend some time discussing how light makes the clock visible. After discussion with the class, they have to devise an experiment to test their ideas. The following is an extract which reflects some of the genuine scientific thinking that has gone on.

Worksheet   Name: ....

How I think we both see the clock:

4.2 Worksheet on vision produced by Leicestershire group of SSCR

<u>The aim of our experiments</u>
The purpose of our tests is to see which drawing is the best of these two (figure 4.3).

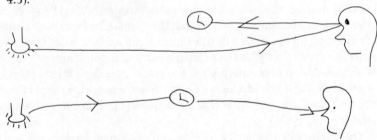

4.3 Children's model of vision

We are trying to find out whether we see things with the light going to the person then the clock or the light going to the clock and then the person. We got a circuit board and an object like a bunch of keys. Then we blocked the light going from the bulb to the keys and the keys went dull. Next we blocked the light from the bulb to our eye. The keys still looked bright.
<u>What we decided</u>
We decided that this is the best one (figure 4.4).

4.4 Children's conclusion about vision

61

We think it is the best one because on the other one if you block the light out that is going to your eye you can still see the object brightly so you don't need the line. If you take the line away then you are left with the drawing above so that is the best one.

Other means of challenging the conceptions they may have about light are the following.

(a) *Using the laser*[5]. The beam is invisible, yet the spot is clearly visible. Pupils should be asked to explain how the light has travelled from the back to the front of the room. The real difficulty comes when chalk dust is scattered in the beam and pupils are asked to explain how the chalk dust makes the light visible.

(b) *Using a light meter to measure the presence of light.* Light from an intense light source at the back of the room can be reflected off a mirror towards the pupils. This will probably produce explanations that the mirror 'bounces' the light back. The mirror can then be replaced with a piece of paper and children asked if this is 'bouncing light off'. Many children think that the light stops on the paper. However a light meter placed within half a metre of the paper, will sense the scattered light and this will be difficult to explain for children who hold this idea.

(c) One of the more interesting discussions to have with pupils is why the moon shines. Many have never considered the problem before and will genuinely advance speculations that it is because it is 'like a light bulb'. This is an excellent question to set to groups in small discussion and ask them to explain their ideas to the rest after five minutes.

The development of a full understanding necessitates the individual internalising the scientific conception of *how they see*. That this is essential for later work will become apparent when the formation of real and virtual images is examined; for example, a virtual image is caused by the fact that rays of light enter the eye *as if* they had come from a particular point. Since the mechanism of sight is due to rays entering the eye it will appear as if the object is at this point. However if a child does not understand the latter idea about the nature of vision, they have very little chance of understanding the concept of virtual images.

The traditional approach here is to move to image-forming devices starting with the simplest of these, the pinhole camera. Modern society makes extensive use of such devices in film and video cameras, microscopes, telescopes and film projectors. It is a good exercise to ask the children to think of as many devices as they can that make use of light to form and record pictures. What features do they all have in common? The word image is not one that is extensively understood by children of this age and it is better to start with the word 'picture' and introduce 'image' as the scientific word for picture.

The pinhole camera

The pinhole camera is an enchanting device, the magic of which has never ceased to charm children. The standard approach is to use it with a filament light bulb and examine the effect of varying the object–camera distance. In addition, let the children 'pepper' the front with lots of small holes

which has the effect of producing multiple images of the filament. It is important to try and provide an opportunity to obtain an image of the outside world
on the screen of the camera lest it is seen as a peculiar artefact of the physics
laboratory. This takes some care as the room has to be kept fairly dark and small
holes provided in the blinds to point the camera at the outside world. After
providing an opportunity to explore, ask the children how the camera 'sees' the
outside world. For instance an interesting question to ask is 'Is the image
coloured?' Children who advance the explanation that the camera actively
takes something from the outside world[6] will have difficulty explaining the
formation of an image on the greaseproof screen, particularly why it is upside
down (figure 4.5).

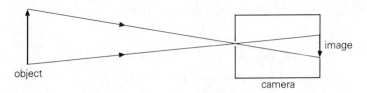

4.5 Pinhole camera

Yet despite the simplicity of the device many children find difficulty in
correctly explaining how the camera works. This is generally because they lack
an appreciation of the fact that light falling on the objects is scattered in all
directions. This needs to be emphasised in discussion if the understanding is not
to descend to the ritualistic reiteration of figure 4.5. The camera should also be
used to show the effect of a lens by enlarging the pinhole so that a fuzzy image is
produced which is made sharp by the lens. Most children miss the equally
important point here that the image becomes brighter and there is more detail
visible. A computer-assisted learning package, *Camera*[7], helps in illustrating
the workings of the pinhole camera and the effect of adding a lens by providing
graphic illustrations under user control.

It would be a pity to miss the opportunity here of introducing children to
simple photography with the pinhole camera. There can be few activities that
are so captivating as introducing children to simple photography. Children can
construct a simple pinhole camera from a modern fizzy drink can and basic
materials that can be found in the home (fig. 4.6). The cameras can be loaded in
a dark room with photographic paper and the exposure performed by poking a
hole through the aluminium foil and leaving the camera static for approximately 10 minutes.

Access to a dark room with a red light is needed and three baths of developer,
fixer and wash. The results will be a negative (white where it should be black
and vice versa) and generally fuzzy image. This does not seem to trouble
children who find the process fascinating.

The pictures produced by pinhole cameras make a useful starting point for
the study of images. Pupils are asked to investigate lenses and see if they can use
them to produce a picture on a translucent screen (greaseproof paper)[8]. This
image is interpreted as 'real' because it can be captured on a piece of paper and it
is definitely there. Such an image is produced by the slide or cinema projector.

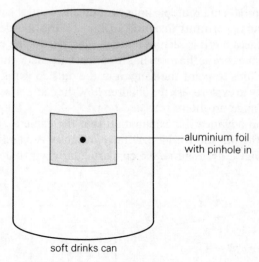

aluminium foil
with pinhole in

soft drinks can

4.6 Simple pinhole camera made from soft drinks can

Explaining its formation is inevitably dependent on introducing the 'ray box' which limits the number of rays incident on the lens. With these, pupils can be asked to investigate what happens to the ray incident at the top, middle and bottom of the lens and then to try all three simultaneously with a triple slit. The essential point is that the rays are recombined to create a picture of the object on the screen. Every point on the image has an equivalent point on the object and the rays genuinely come together here rather than just appearing to. Again, in explaining the phenomenon, it is important to emphasise that the three rays chosen are an extremely limited subset of the many rays that are scattered by the object.

Further treatment of telescopes and microscopes is really beyond the scope of this book. However, providing that the fundamentals of light have been understood, pupils should find most standard treatments comprehensible. The one device worth spending some time on here is the camera. This is a device familiar to most and as such generally interests pupils. A brief discussion of the merits and disadvantages of the main types is useful. The important point to bring out, preferably with a selection of cameras to hand, is the common features; a box, a lens, a shutter and a film.

Virtual images

The study of virtual images is best introduced through mirrors with which children are very familiar. Children should be asked to try and answer three questions:

(a) where is the picture you see of yourself in the mirror (on, in front or behind the mirror)?
(b) how could you prove it?
(c) why is the writing in a mirror the wrong way around?

Answering these three questions needs an understanding that objects scatter light in all directions and that the angle of incidence of a ray equals the angle of reflection. This is one concept that children generally seem happy to accept, possibly because of their experiences with tennis balls. Pupils can then be asked to use this idea to solve the puzzles presented initially. It is important to know that a large number of children hold the opinion that the image they see in the mirror is on the surface of the mirror and not behind it. This means that the answer to this problem should be surprising to them and the teacher will need to recognise this and allow time for discussion.

The point we are ultimately hoping children will understand is that the image in the mirror is not on the surface but that our eyes are deluded into thinking that the rays we see come from an object which appears to be equidistant behind the mirror. This is what we call a 'virtual image' as the image is not really there. Guesne[9] has pointed to the fact that the lack of a correct model of vision is one of the possible reasons that pupils will have difficulty in understanding the notion of a virtual image. She makes an important point about figure 4.7.

> 'The physicist interprets the virtual image of object O in a mirror by saying that the light reaches the eye of the observer after having been deflected by the mirror exactly as if it came in a straight line from object O' ... This model then rests on the idea that the object is seen because the light comes from it and that it penetrates our eye after having been propagated in a straight line in the intermediate space.'

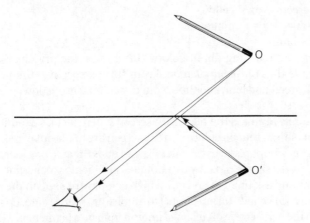

4.7 Diagram showing image formation by a mirror

Children who do not see vision in terms of light entering the eye will have substantial difficulty understanding the nature of a virtual image. They will not be able to explain why the eye thinks that there is another object behind the mirror which is not really there. Little recognition of this difficulty is given by traditional explanations and in the discussion afterwards it will be worth stressing.

Colour

As a topic, this benefits from the healthy egocentric interest of most pupils based on their wealth of experience. However, most physics teachers approach it with a substantial amount of caution. Primarily, this is because the topic has already been extensively explored by pupils with paint boxes for many years prior to their arrival in the science classroom. These lessons have taught them that the three primary colours are

○ red   which a scientist would call   magenta
○ yellow
○ blue   which a scientist would call   cyan (turquoise)

All colours can be produced by mixing a combination of these paints. However, colour theory is often confused because there are two perspectives and it is essential to be clear about which one is being used. Firstly, there is the theory of *colour subtraction* which applies to pigments (paints). For pigments, the primary colours are magenta, cyan and yellow. Pigments have their colour because they act as filters absorbing all the colours in white light except the colour of the pigment itself. Therefore a red book looks red because the pigment in the paper absorbs all the light in white light apart from red. This process is described as colour subtraction by scientists as the pigment subtracts colours from white light.

However, coloured light can be directly *added* to produce the whole spectrum of colours. The three primary colours for *colour addition* are red, green and blue. Adding these colours together by shining them onto the same spot gives what are called the secondary colours.

○ red + green   =   yellow
○ red + blue   =   magenta
○ green + blue   =   cyan

In discussing and teaching about colours in physics, the principal theory being discussed is that of *colour addition*. From this perspective, the primary colours are red, green and blue and the secondary colours are yellow, magenta and cyan.

The best example of this is the television screen where a close examination with a hand lens shows that all colours on the screen are made out of red, green and blue. The eye cannot resolve these details and adds them to produce all the other colours. A very simple but effective home experiment is to provide pupils with a hand lens and ask them to find out which colours are used on the screen to make (*a*) white, (*b*) yellow, (*c*) purple, (*d*) turquoise, (*e*) red, (*f*) blue, (*g*) green.

Viewed from the perspective of *colour addition*, a magenta pigment or filter is a combination of two primary colours, red and blue. Therefore it will allow these two colours to pass through it, which the eye adds to produce the secondary colour magenta. The primary colour it will not pass is green and for this reason it is sometimes referred to as a minus green pigment or filter. Extending this to the other pigments we have:

○ magenta   is equivalent to   − green
○ yellow   is equivalent to   − blue
○ cyan   is equivalent to   − red

Mixing magenta pigment with yellow pigment has the effect of providing two filters and removing (subtracting) green and blue so the resulting colour perceived is red. This can be seen clearly with a white light viewed through a magenta and yellow filter.

Not surprisingly, the introduction of these ideas to children is a positive oasis of confusion as the scientific stance is contrary to all their experience and intuition.

Changing children's understanding can only be achieved by a variety of clear demonstrations and experiences. A good medium of exploration though, are computer programs which provide a dynamic illustration of the mixing of colours. *Colours*[10] is a good example of these, allowing children or the teacher to mix any combinations of three colours. Children can then examine closely the detailed spots on the screen that are being used to make the specific colours. Another very effective demonstration is to use three slide projectors. Into each projector is inserted a good quality primary colour slide with a circular mask of black paper attached to the surface. Each slide is projected onto a white screen so that the colours overlap as in figure 4.8.

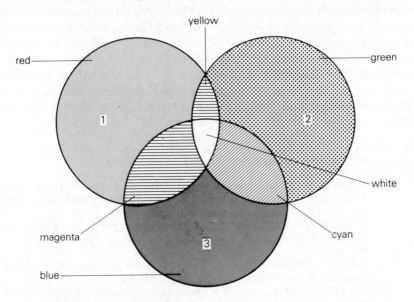

4.8 Mixing of coloured lights

This demonstration is not easy. It requires three slide projectors of equal luminosity but it provides a clear demonstration of the principle. An alternative method of demonstration is to use three ray boxes with independent power supplies for each box. The 'blue' bulb needs to be run at a higher voltage (15 V) to provide an adequate blue. This leads suitably to the question. 'If we can make white light by adding red, blue and green, can we split white light into colours?' After a discussion of rainbows and thin films on puddles, this is a useful opportunity to produce the ray boxes and the prisms and challenge the pupils to see if they, like Newton, can split the white light into colours. This experimental session is best completed by a demonstration of the production of a spectrum in as dark a room as possible. This is most effective if a slide projector is used as the light source with a high dispersion prism to produce the spectrum. The demonstration is one of the many 'pretty' experiments of physics that never ceases to charm pupils. Pupils may argue that they can only see six colours of the spectrum as it is impossible to distinguish the indigo from violet. The seven colours of the rainbow were settled upon by Newton who had a superstitious belief in the number seven. Most people can agree on red, orange, yellow, green, blue and violet, and indigo is practically impossible for most people to pick out.

Finally, this is a good point to return to the colour filters. If white light is really made out of colours, we should be able to select out just one light. This can be shown with any colour filter. However Andersson & Kärrqvist[2] have shown that a substantial number of children believe that filters *add* colour to the light. Fortunately this is easy to test. If filters add colour, passing a white beam through a red filter, followed by a green filter should add these colours to the light and the resulting light should be some combination of these colours when viewed from the other side. However what happens in reality, providing reasonable quality filters are used, is that the first filter only transmits red light which is not able to pass through the green so no light is transmitted. If this is presented to pupils as a challenge to explain, it should challenge the concept outlined above. The computer-assisted learning package *Colours*[10] provides a clear and effective illustration of these ideas. If there are still those that doubt the action of a filter, laser light could be passed through a blue filter in an attempt to colour it blue. The failure of this experiment should convince most pupils.

Notes and references

1 Guesne E. (1978) 'Lumière et vision des objets: un example de representation des phenomenes preexistant a l'enseignment.' In *Physics Teaching in Schools*, pp. 265–73. Taylor and Francis, London.
2 Andersson B. & Kärrqvist C. (1983) 'How Swedish pupils aged 12–15 years understand light and its properties.' *European Journal of Science Education*, **5** (4), 387–402.
3 Stead B.F. & Osborne R.J. (1980) 'Exploring science students' concept of light.' *Australian Science Teachers Journal*, **26** (3), 84–90.
4 Crookes J. & Goldby G. (1948) in *Science as a Process. Encouraging the scientific activity of children*, pp. 71–85. Leicestershire Education Authority.
5 Before using the laser you should read the DES memorandum. 'The use of lasers in schools.' Lasers are quite safe as long as **you do not look down the beam**. It is possible that this can happen accidentally if there are metal reflective surfaces present. These should be removed beforehand.
6 Susan Sontag in her book *On Photography*, Penguin 1979, explains how Balzac saw the body as a succession of ghostly images and objected to photographs as he saw the camera as 'laying hold' and removing one of these images. Many primitive tribes are noted for similarly objecting to photographs as it steals some of their spirit.
7 *Camera*. Science in Process Software. Capital Media, ILECC, John Ruskin St, London SE5.
8 See Revised Nuffield Physics, Teachers Guide Year III, p. 39–40, for further details.
9 Guesne E. (1985) 'Light.' In *Children's Ideas in Science*. (eds. Driver R., Guesne E. & Tiberghien A.), Open University Press, Milton Keynes.
10 *Colours*. Science in Process Software. Capital Media, ILECC, John Ruskin St, London SE5.

5 Kinetic theory

Particles

Since the time of the Greeks, people have believed in the concept of matter being constructed from particles. Feynman[1] aptly illustrates what a powerful idea this is in this quote.

> 'If, in some cataclysm, all scientific knowledge were to be destroyed, what statement would contain the most information in the fewest words? I believe it is the atomic hypothesis that all things are made of atoms – little particles that move around in perpetual motion.'

However, the evidence for this belief is indirect and has to be inferred from experiments such as those which demonstrate Brownian motion and diffusion. But, it is remarkably successful at predicting the behaviour of solids, liquids and gases. Childrens' appreciation that matter may be particulate most probably comes from playing with sand or dust which provides first hand experience of the fine division of matter.

Some of the most significant research work of childrens' ideas has been done by the Children's Learning in Science Project.[2] The project team set a series of questions that required an understanding of the kinetic theory to answer them satisfactorily. They found the following range of ideas expressed by children of ages 12–14:

(a) particles themselves change in size as the temperature changes;

(b) particles themselves melt when a solid changes to a liquid (that is, particles themselves have the properties of bulk material);

(c) particles are attributed with anthropomorphic qualities, i.e. 'they prefer to go into a vacuum because it's less crowded';

(d) the particles are not necessarily in continuous motion, they stop on cooling or at 0 °C;

(e) the space between particles is not empty, a commonly-held view is that it is full of air:

(f) there are forces between the particles and that
   (i) the size of the force changes with temperature,
   (ii) the force between the particles contribute to pressure,
   (iii) the force between the particles gets weaker as the temperature increases;

(g) the exact nature of the particle motion is confused: particles in solids are seen as free to move and those in liquids are said to be vibrating.

Nussbaum & Novick[3] found that although 78% of the children they interviewed could correctly identify the particulate model of a gas, this did not imply that the children had the correct understanding of other aspects of this model.

Only half were able to say decisively that this implied that there was empty space between the particles and 15% believed that the particles would be concentrated in one area. Again, only half ascribed the particles with any intrinsic motion.

The implication of all this for teachers is that children arrive with stable models that need to be recognised and challenged. Initially it is a good idea to allow children an opportunity, either by discussion, some writing or drawing a poster to express their ideas. Imaginative exercises are often helpful here. Suggest that they are in an accident and when they wake up, they are perfectly alright but the air has become visible? What would they see?

Nussbaum[4] suggests using the apparatus shown in figure 5.1 as an 'exposing event' which allows children to define their model. After demonstrating the

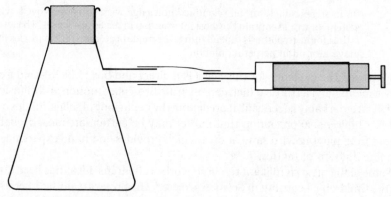

5.1 Apparatus for testing particle ideas about air

effect of the syringe, it is attached to the flask and some of the air removed. The pupils are asked to suggest how the air would look through magic eye glasses. Most of the suggested models represent air as a continuous substance with no gaps and with some portion of the flask left empty. Discussion can then be held as to where the gap will be sited. Pupils can then be shown a 'discrepant' event. Air in a syringe is compressed to half or quarter of its original volume. How can this be explained if there are no gaps between the particles? Nussbaum suggests that a few will suggest the idea that air naturally contains 'empty spaces' and the group are well prepared to accept the idea that there are spaces between the particles in air.

These ideas can be explored further by demonstrating diffusion using any particularly strong perfume. The children can be asked to explain how the smell reaches them. Another interesting experiment is the diffusion of ammonia and hydrogen chloride. This can be done with the apparatus shown in figure 5.2, though care is needed to avoid filling the room with ammonia.

White ammonium chloride is formed where the two gases meet. An interesting aspect of this experiment is that, because of the differing speeds of the particles involved, the ring is not formed in the centre.

A novel aspect of the teaching of this subject is that it is the first time that explicit reference is made to a 'theory'. What we are doing is presenting a model of reality that allows us to explain experimental observations and make

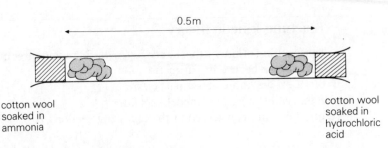

0.5m

cotton wool
soaked in
ammonia

cotton wool
soaked in
hydrochloric
acid

5.2 Apparatus to demonstrate diffusion

predictions about the behaviour of gases which can be tested. The kinetic theory is based on three premises:
- ○ that particles behave as hard spherical objects;
- ○ that these particles collide elastically* with each other;
- ○ the range of the attractive and repulsive forces between the particles is small compared to the mean distance between them.

Warren[5] has argued that teachers are guilty of deception here in that the results of kinetic theory can be derived without either of the first two assumptions, which are also untrue. However, the point of this exercise is to show that a simple mechanical model of matter has substantial explanatory power of physical phenomena. An improved model would not be comprehensible to pupils of this age and is unnecessary. Unfortunately physics teaching is riddled with conceptual models that the mature physicist could not accept. This is inevitable, as the evidence is that children do not have the mental ability to cope with the formal abstractions necessary to understand some of these ideas.

This is a valuable opportunity to emphasise to children the nature of scientific theories as descriptors of reality. The theory is satisfactory and accepted, within its limitations, because it is successful in explaining our observations. This does not mean that it is a 'true' picture of reality and that particles are hard round solid objects; they merely behave as if they were. A more sophisticated picture is the Rutherford model of the atom which sees the atom as containing a very small massive nucleus consisting of protons and neutrons with the electrons a very long way away orbiting the nucleus. However such a picture is not acceptable to the quantum physicist, as it implies that nuclear particles are solid objects whose position and momentum can be accurately defined. They would say that you can only talk of the probability of an electron being in a particular position at a certain instant. The view of atoms as hard solid spheres is not 'correct', but in this instant is adequate to make powerful predictions. This may seem an abstract point but it is easy to give the impression in teaching physics that we are presenting absolute known facts about the world. It is important to guard against this deception. Chalmers[6] provides a fascinating introduction to the nature of science with particular emphasis on physics.

Note that the theory is stated in terms of *particles*. This is the preferred term that should be used instead of atoms, molecules or ions. It is too easy to lapse into the wrong terminology and add to the pupil's confusion.

---

* An elastic collision is one where the kinetic energy of the particles is conserved.

Teaching kinetic theory

The teaching of kinetic theory addresses the following three questions.
(*a*) Why do we believe in particles?
(*b*) What do we know about particles?
(*c*) What will the particle model explain?
These questions are considered in the following sections.

Why do we believe in particles?

There are a variety of experiments or demonstrations that can be performed here. None of these 'prove' the existence of particles but they support the concept.

(*a*) *Air occupies space*. Bubbling air from a syringe into an inverted test tube full of water pushes the water out. This shows that there is something to a gas.

(*b*) *Air has weight*. The simplest way to demonstrate this is with a one litre flask which can be weighed on an electronic balance that measures to ± 0.1 g. The flask is weighed and then evacuated with a pump. The rubber tubing connecting it to the pump is then sealed with a Hoffman clip and the flask is reweighed. The difference in weight is the weight of 1 litre of air. This needs to be done behind a safety screen in case of an implosion.

(*c*) *Particles can be poured*. A beaker of sand pours as if it was a liquid. Children can be asked to pour a beaker of sand and compare it with pouring a beaker of water. Ask the children what the pouring of the sand would look like if the particles were even smaller. This analogy can be taken even further by the use of a 'fluidised bed'. This is a container of salt or sand through which air is blown. The sand behaves and feels like a liquid under such conditions, and objects can be 'floated' on the top. There is an excellent example of a large-scale fluidised bed at *Launch Pad*[7] at the Science Museum which clearly demonstrates the concept of a liquid consisting of particles in motion.

(*d*) *Crystals can be grown and crystals of one substance all have the same shape*. This can be done quickly under a microscope with saturated salt solution or over a longer period with copper sulphate crystals. If the time is available the latter is preferable because of the fun of this experiment. Children become fascinated with the beautiful shapes and compete with each other to grow the largest crystal. Discuss with the children why all the crystals have the same shape. How could this be explained? An explanation in terms of particles that pack together in the same way each time like the greengrocer's oranges provides a suitable model. This is easily demonstrated with polystyrene balls.

(*e*) *Laue X-ray photographs of crystals can be circulated*. The exact symmetry of the X-ray photograph is a reflection of an internal order within the crystal. This is more effectively done if a set of the Nuffield A-level Chemistry photographic grids are used to observe a point source of light. The grids with a regular arrangement of dots produce regular and symmetrical patterns of light. The argument is then advanced that X-rays incident on atoms produce regular patterns because the atoms are packed in ordered arrangements. However this evidence is indirect and may seem rather remote to children.

Solomon[8] rightly points out that there is not a single school experiment that can be relied upon to convince a sceptical child that all matter consists of the 'hard, massy atoms' of Newton and Dalton. It is much better, as she recommends, to expound the whole theory with conviction rather than rely on inductive generalisations from the scanty evidence that can be presented in the school science laboratory.

What do we know about particles?

The experiment that is normally performed is that of looking at smoke in a cell under a microscope. This demonstrates Brownian motion. It is important to note though that this experiment is a classic case of the necessity of prior knowledge in order to perceive the movement of the particles. Most pupils expect to see two or three rather large spots of light and spend their time looking for this and miss the relevant observation even when they have set up everything perfectly correctly. What they should see is a dark field with a large number of very small bright dots which are moving quickly and randomly. It is strongly recommended that teachers set up a microscope at the front to which pupils can refer as a guide to what they should be able to see, otherwise they often miss the observation totally. Driver[9] has also pointed to the fact that some pupils think that the random motion is caused by the particles bumping into each other. Pupils should be posed the challenge of testing whether this is true. Do the particles only change direction when they bump into each other or do they apparently change direction spontaneously and at random?

Other indirect evidence that supports the concept that gases consist of particles moving at high speed comes from experiments with diffusion. These are best done with bromine because it is a clearly visible gas, but teachers *must* follow the recommended safety procedures[10]. The bromine is released initially into a sealed glass vessel containing air. The bromine normally takes about 30 minutes to diffuse to the top, but it shows clearly that the particles are moving. Pupils can then be asked to speculate how fast they think the individual particles are moving? How could we devise an experiment to measure the speed of bromine particles on their own with no air present?

This is done by releasing bromine into a vacuum. Discussion should be held with the pupils before breaking the vial as to how long they think it will take the gas to reach the top. The almost instantaneous result in which the bromine rushes to the top generally surprises most pupils. Indirect evidence that particles do move this fast comes from measuring the speed of sound. The value can be measured directly by timing the speed of pulse of sound over a meter with modern apparatus.[11] Children could be asked to stand in a line, pass a note along and think what decides how fast the note reaches the other end. Hopefully a clear link will be made showing that the speed of the pulse is merely a reflection of the speed of the individual particles.

73

These experiments are the principal evidence used to establish our belief in the theory. Pupils find the model of the drunkard trying to walk home a useful analogy and if time is available this can be modelled with a small LOGO[12] program.

```
TO WANDER
REPEAT 100[FORWARD 10 SETHEADING PICK 360]
END
```

This program causes the turtle to take 100 steps of length 10 units. Before it takes each step it randomly picks the heading from a 360 degree angle. The distance travelled directly can be compared with the actual distance gone. Theory predicts that, if the particle is moving totally randomly, after 100 steps it should be on average, $\sqrt{100}$ steps from its starting point, i.e. a distance equal to $\sqrt{100} \times 10$ from its starting point.

The common pieces of apparatus used to illustrate the kinetic model are a tray with marbles and the '3D kinetic model'. The former has to be carefully introduced if it is not to become a session where marbles are scattered wildly around the room. The latter is much better, consisting of ball bearings in a perspex cylinder driven by a motorised plate at the bottom. A vivid demonstration of the behaviour of smoke particles is presented when a large piece of polystyrene is added. Pupils should be told to concentrate on the polystyrene which represents the smoke particles and imagine that the ball bearings are invisible. The effect is more dramatic if the lights are dimmed so that the ball bearings do become invisible. In performing this demonstration using ball bearings to represent the particles we begin to explore the third question.

What will the particle model explain?

Kinetic theory successfully explains why gases are able to exert a pressure. The idea of gases exerting pressure is often introduced with dramatic experiments such as the collapsing can experiment. A vacuum pump removes the air from a large metal can which is crushed by the pressure of the air. Most pupils explain this using a concept of 'suction' which, although erroneous, is remarkably successful at explaining why liquids rise up straws and how vacuum cleaners work. This concept fails to explain why a card should remain on an inverted glass full of water. Similarly if a long tube (10 m) is filled with water and then unravelled keeping one end in a bucket of water and the other end clamped, the water will be supported in the tube to a height of approximately 10 m (figure 5.3).

The latter experiment is far preferable to the same demonstration with mercury in a tube because of the dangers of using mercury and the enlarged scale of the effect. Both experiments are extremely difficult to explain without introducing the scientific idea that the air is exerting a pressure which is supporting the water in the beaker and the tube.

The '3D kinetic model' is very good for explaining why a gas is able to exert a pressure. A large piece of polystyrene is inserted into the tube so that it only just fits in the tube. When the model is set in motion, the 'pressure' of the particles

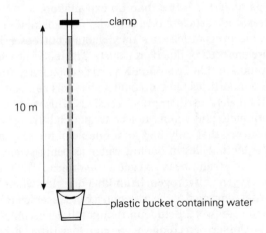

10 m

clamp

plastic bucket containing water

5.3 Apparatus to show the strength of atmospheric pressure

bombarding the polystyrene lifts it upwards. At an introductory level it is sufficient to provide the explanation that the pressure of the gas is caused by the bombardment of the walls by the particles. A fuller explanation would use Newton's Third Law to explain it. The particles colliding with the wall exert a force on the wall which can be detected as the pressure of the gas. The walls of the container exert an equal force in the opposite direction of the gas particles which produces a change in momentum of the particle. On the large scale, a direct experience of this can be provided by throwing a tennis ball at the back of a pupil volunteer. Thrown with reasonable vigour, the pupil will normally move forward as a result of the force exerted on them by the ball. With a more able group this can be developed to derive the formula for a pressure of gas

$$pV = \tfrac{1}{3}Nmc^2$$

This is consistent with the equation for an ideal gas $pV = RT$ which is an empirical result. The provision of an explanatory theoretical model represented a triumph for the kinetic theory. Teachers who do not wish to derive the expression are advised to simply state it. The formula allows a comparison of the two equations to be made and the observation that it can be written in the form

$$pV = \tfrac{2}{3}N \times \tfrac{1}{2}mc^2$$

Comparing this with the gas equation, it is apparent that the kinetic energy of the particles ($\tfrac{1}{2}mc^2$) is a *measure* of the temperature of the gas. This is commonly used to provide an explanation of the concept of an absolute zero of temperature. This is the temperature at which particle motion has totally ceased and hence a lower temperature cannot be achieved. This would be true for an ideal gas but not any real substance as it would contradict Heisenberg's uncertainty principle[13]. To teach that particle motion is zero at absolute zero is fallacious, but this is the only simplistic reduction that is comprehensible by pupils. Some explanation of this curious phenomenon of a finite lower temperature is necessary and as such it is better than no explanation.

Moving on from gases, the particle model provides an explanation of the nature of a liquid. The concept of particles in random motion but loosely held in a semi-ordered structure has been outlined previously. The model provides an explanation for evaporation in that occasionally particles break free from the surface of the liquid. Such particles have become a gas. This can be demonstrated with the 2D/3D 'models' used on prior occasions. This is not an easy idea for children to assimilate and should not be treated lightly. Osborne & Cosgrove[14] found in a survey that only 28% of a sample of 86 15-year-olds could correctly describe the bubbles in boiling water as being steam when offered five alternatives, air, steam, heat, oxygen or hydrogen. The majority believed that they were oxygen or hydrogen. In another question where pupils were asked to explain what happened to the water on a wet saucer left to dry on the drainage board of a sink, 45% of the students thought that it became 'bits of water' in the air and a similar percentage were convinced that it became oxygen or hydrogen. The rest thought it no longer existed.

The implication of this is that teachers should investigate whether any of their class are operating with these 'alternative' models. If the particle model of a liquid is true then it should be possible to recover the particles by slowing them down and creating a liquid again. Pupils who hold alternative views will experience difficulty supplying a plausible hypothesis to explain how the water reappears.

For a solid, the particle model explains the regular structure of crystals, the Von Laue X-ray diffraction patterns and photographs obtained with a field ion microscope such as in figure 5.4. In addition it provides an understanding of

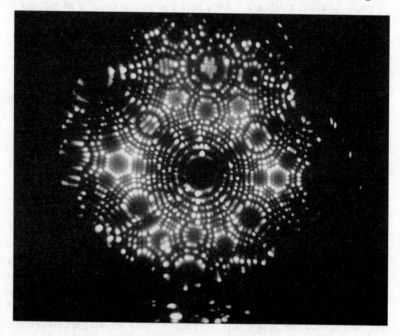

5.4 Field ion micrograph of iridium

why solids, liquids and gases expand when heated. The effect of warming a solid would be to provide the particles with more internal energy which would cause them to vibrate more rapidly about their mean position and effectively occupy more space. This would imply that we would expect a solid to expand as the temperature increases and there are many experiments that demonstrate this. One of the most effective is to use a long strip of aluminium cooking foil set against a screen of diagonal stripes which help to provide a clear background against which movement can easily be perceived (figure 5.5). The foil is suspended between two retort stands and heated by several candles beneath.

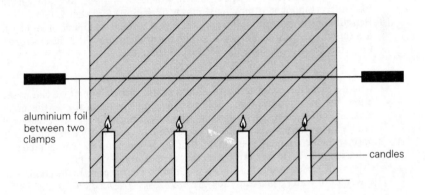

aluminium foil between two clamps

candles

5.5 Apparatus to show expansion of metal on heating

The expansion of the foil is sufficient to show a very distinctive sag in the metal as it is heated by the candles. This is a delightful experiment, of the 'sealing wax and string' variety, which shows the expansion of metals more effectively than many other experiments to be found in the textbooks.

Notes and references

1 Feynman R. (1964) *Lectures on Physics*, vol. 1, 1–2. Addison Wesley.
2 Brooks, Briggs and Driver (1984) *Children's Understanding of the Particulate Nature of Matter*, CLIS Project, Leeds.
3 Novick S. & Nussbaum J. (1978) 'Junior high school pupil's understanding of the particulate nature of matter: an interview study.' *Science Education*, **62 (3)**, 273–81.
4 Nussbaum J. (1985) 'The Particulate Nature of Matter in the Gaseous Phase', in *Children's Ideas in Science*, eds. R. Driver, E. Guesne & A. Tiberghien. Open University Press, Milton Keynes.
5 Warren J. (1965) *The Teaching of Physics*. Butterworths, London.
6 Chalmers, A. (1982) *What is This Thing Called Science?* (2nd ed.) Open University Press, Milton Keynes.
7 The *Launch Pad* is a new gallery (1986) introduced by the Science Museum, London, to provide children with a phenomenological experience of many of the facets of science. There are over 70 exhibits which are all interactive and many illustrate fundamental principles of physics. Their primary aim is to be motivational rather than didactic. The visit provides a very enjoyable experi-

ence for pupils of all ages and is highly recommended. At the time of writing, similar exhibitions can be found at the *Exploratorium* in Bristol and in Cardiff.

8 Solomon J. (1980) *Teaching Children in the Laboratory*. Croom Helm, London.

9 Driver R. (1983) *The Pupil as Scientist?* Open University Press, Milton Keynes.

10 Unfortunately bromine is a poisonous substance which attacks the skin and lungs. Experiments with bromine are quite safe providing the standard safety routines are followed. These are outlined in *Revised Nuffield Physics Teacher's Guide, Year III*, pp. 166–7.

11 The Unilab Ratemeter and the VELA with the physics EPROM both have the facility to time pulses of sound from a microphone directly and yield extremely accurate results. Older methods of doing this experiment rely on using an oscilloscope as a timer and will take a little longer to become familiar with.

12 This program is written using LCSI LOGO which is commonly available on the BBC microcomputer. It may need minor alterations for other LOGOs.

13 Heisenberg's uncertainty principle states that if the coordinates of an object are known to an uncertainty of $\pm \Delta x$ and the momentum of the object with an uncertainty of $\pm \Delta p$, then the product of these two

$$\Delta x \Delta p \geqslant h$$

where h is Planck's constant. According to this principle then we can never know the exact state of any object with complete accuracy as the more accurate one measurement becomes, the less accurate is the other. Hence if our particles were at rest it would be possible to completely determine their position which would necessitate that their momentum was completely indeterminate if Heisenberg's principle were to remain valid.

14 Osborne R.J. & Cosgrove M.M. (1983) 'Children's conception of the changes of the state of water'. *Journal of Research in Science Teaching*, **20**, **9**, 825–38.

6 Waves

Any understanding of modern science requires a knowledge of waves and wave behaviour. Most of our sensory experiences as adults depends on waves: light waves to see, sound waves to hear, radio waves to carry visual and auditory information, electrical and microwaves to transmit our telephone conversations. Hence most physics courses provide an introduction to wave behaviour and properties, often starting in the third year. Little research has been done into the nature of children's ideas about waves[1]. However children's experiences of water in the bath and the sea does provide them with some basis for their ideas. The most common misconception is that the wave is a physical lump of water that travels across the surface. It is worth starting the subject by asking the pupils to list as many items as possible that they know of that use waves and to draw a picture of a water wave and a sound wave to provide a basis for further discussion. The BBC Science Topics series has a video of waves[2] that provides a useful introduction to the topic.

Introducing wave behaviour

Teaching of the subject of waves usually starts with an exploration of wave behaviour on springs. There are two types of springs commonly in use for this, a tightly coiled fairly massive spring, about 2 m in length, and the Slinky. The latter is very suitable for demonstration but not for use by pupils as it easily ties itself in knots. Pupils can perform set exercises with these springs to explore the factors determining wave speed, what happens to waves that cross and what happens to a wave on reflection. Essentially this is an exercise in observation which pupils enjoy but find difficult to draw the correct conclusions. It shows that the wave speed is independent of the size of the wave (the amplitude) but is dependent on the tension in the spring. The more difficult point to spot is that the waves actually cross when a single wave (a pulse) is transmitted simultaneously from each end. This is more likely to be seen successfully if one pulse is sent as a 'down' pulse and the other as an 'up' pulse as in figure 6.1. The pupils must then be asked which pulse gets to the other end? If they do 'bounce off' each other, which is the commonly held view, the waves would return to their originating end; if not, they have crossed through each other. Further evidence that waves do genuinely cross can be provided by producing two ripples on a large tank or in a bath at home!

A similar technique is necessary to discover what happens to a pulse on reflection. The pupils should look closely to see whether an 'up' pulse returns as an 'up' pulse or has been inverted to a 'down' pulse. Pulses are inverted on reflection. Pupil observation will have to be directed to this phenomenon if

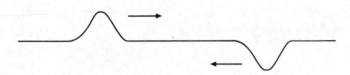

6.1 Two pulses on a spring

pupils are to spot it in their general enjoyment of the apparatus. Finally the pupils can be asked to create a 'standing wave'. Generally, this is something they discover without much prompting, but they could be asked to speculate as to why this wave should appear to be standing still.

From these activities the physics teacher begins to develop the language used to describe a wave. Useful terms to introduce and define are amplitude, wavelength and frequency. The definition of the latter two can be usefully illustrated with the scales on radios. Fortunately VHF/FM scales are marked in the frequency of the wave, while medium wave and long wave are marked in the wavelength in metres. The introduction of the unit hertz is a useful opportunity to discuss the history of radio and the importance of Hertz's and others' work.

Hertz is generally credited with the discovery of radio waves in 1888. However this popular interpretation is an oversimplification. Hertz would not have been able to interpret his observation, that the electric sparks he was creating were discharging a sphere on the opposite side of the room, if it had not been for Maxwell. Maxwell had predicted theoretically the existence of electromagnetic waves in 1864. Hertz used his 'discovery' to develop a spark transmitter and to investigate the nature of these waves. The development of radio is generally credited to Marconi who was the first person to develop a successful transmitter which he used to transmit from his loft to the garden shed. He then successfully transmitted morse code over longer and longer distances, the English Channel followed by the Irish Channel. Then in 1901, he attempted to transmit across the Atlantic. At the time, most people thought that he had little chance of success as the waves were known to travel in straight lines. Hence it was inconceivable that they could possibly 'curve around' the Earth. Fortunately for Marconi, his experiment worked at the first attempt because of the existence of the ionosphere. This is a region surrounding the Earth where charged particles from the Sun are trapped because of the Earth's magnetic field whose existence was unknown in 1901. Marconi had been lucky and his hunch had paid off. Again, it is worth noting that Marconi was dependent for his success on the lesser-known developments that had led to the invention of vacuum tubes with metal–glass seals that allowed valves to be made.

The history of science provides a useful illustration of science as a human activity. The problem with much of it is that it is a simplification of the processes of history. Posterity credits individuals with discoveries, for instance 'James Watt discovered the steam engine'. However this is a gross simplification: Watt did not discover the steam engine as others, such as Newcomen, had already made working steam engines. Watt's achievement was to develop a separate compartment for condensing the steam which made the steam engine substantially more efficient. Watt, just like ourselves, was dependent on the technology of the time, and the modern steam engine is the result of many people's creative efforts. Science teachers often act as 'Whig' historians in that they present the history of science as a succession of successful discoveries ignoring the failures and the blind alleys necessary for one individual to succeed. One author[3] has described Newton as 'the master of the fudge factor himself' since Newton invented a term called 'the crassitude of the air' which he used rather arbitrarily in deriving an explanation for the speed of sound in air. Science has not been, and never will be, the objective study of nature that is often presented in the textbooks.

This is a good point to illustrate that there are two types of waves, a longitudinal (compression) wave and a transverse wave. Many texts labour the distinction between these two which is fairly obvious. Both waves can be demonstrated with the 'Slinky'. However there are many models available for demonstrating these and two computer programs[4,5] provide a useful demonstration of the two types of wave. Their main advantage is that they allow one particle to be highlighted so that the pupils can clearly see that the particles merely oscillate about a fixed point and do not travel with the wave. In addition, they allow the wavelength and frequency to be adjusted and two waves to be superposed.

Transverse waves cannot be transmitted through the interior of a liquid since the shear (sideways) forces cannot be transmitted from one particle to another. Shear forces are forces which would cause layers of adjacent atoms to move relative to each other. This can be shown clearly with a line of pupils. If they are not holding hands, the only wave that can be transmitted is a compression waves. A study of the waves produced by earthquakes has led to the deduction that the interior of the Earth is still a liquid as transverse waves (the S waves) are not detected on the other side of the Earth (figure 6.2). This is because S wave are transverse waves and therefore can not travel *through* a liquid. The P waves, which are longitudinal waves, can and are detected at all points on the surface of the Earth.

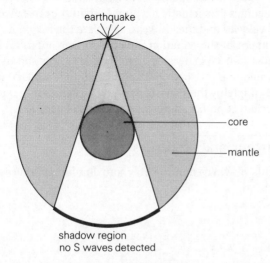

6.2 Transmission of earthquake waves

Sound waves are examples of longitudinal compression waves. Pupils can be asked to consider how the sound produced by the voice reaches the ears of someone on the opposite side of the room. Again, the useful model to consider is that of a line of pupils. The vibrational information can only be transmitted by one molecule colliding with another, that is, one pupil colliding with another. If the air surrounding the source is removed, the object cannot be heard. This is normally done by suspending a bell in an evacuated bell jar. Some care is needed with this experiment if it is to be an effective demonstration, as the bell needs to be suspended from rubber supports which do not transmit any vibration through the solid surfaces of the bell jar and its base.

The concept of frequency is provided with useful reinforcement by testing the range of hearing of the pupils. To do this a signal generator is connected to a loudspeaker and the frequency varied over the complete audible range. This is normally 20–20 000 Hz for most children. However most school loudspeakers cannot respond to the lower frequencies and the lower cut-off point is approximately 50 Hz. A useful way of testing the extremes is to ask the class to stand up. Then gradually raise/lower the frequency and instruct the class to sit down when they can no longer hear the sound. This gives a good visual impression for the whole class and turning the signal generator off surreptitiously soon reveals who is deceiving themselves about the range of their hearing. Children seem to enjoy this experiment as a sense of personal significance can easily be attached to it.

Finally, it is normal to introduce the relationship between wave speed, frequency and wavelength for pupils who are more able. In essence, if the idea is presented intuitively, there is nothing difficult about the following equation.

Wave velocity = frequency × wavelength

For example, if a woman takes four steps a second (the frequency of steps) and each step is 0.5 m large (the wavelength), how far will she have travelled after one second? An alternative analogy is that of a train passing a station. If two carriages go by each second and each is 15 m long, what is the speed of the train? The equation becomes problematic for pupils when they are given the wavelength and wave velocity and then have to calculate the frequency. This necessitates rearrangement of the equation which younger pupils find difficult[6]. A sense of wonder can be generated here by taking the approximate frequency of a local radio station such as Capital Radio (1.5 MHz) and its wavelength (200 m); multiplying these two figures gives a value for the speed of radio waves. It is sufficient if pupils appreciate that this is very fast.

Wave behaviour and properties

Most treatments of waves aim to show four fundamental aspects of wave behaviour which are
- reflection
- refraction
- diffraction
- interference

The apparatus used to demonstrate these effects, the ripple tank, is problematic for most pupils. As Driver[7] has pointed out, it is hard to pick out the salient features from the complex patterns generated in ripple tanks. Yet a misplaced belief in 'discovery learning' has meant that teachers find it hard to point to the aspects that pupils should observe. Most current teachers' guides give the impression that pupils should be allowed to explore the patterns and observe them independently. This tendency is carried to its absurd limit in the apocryphal story told of one early 'Nuffield' teacher who phoned up the organisers after four weeks to ask 'if it was alright after four weeks of experimenting with ripple tanks to tell his pupils that they should put water in them?' In reality, this is not a sensible approach. Pupils benefit if the effects are clearly demonstrated with the apparatus or by other means[2]. One useful method of demonstrating these is to put the lamp *beneath* the tank and project the patterns on the ceiling. In a darkened room this provides an effective large-scale demonstration[8] of the phenomenon. Children's attention can be judiciously drawn to the essential features of the wave patterns obtained in the tank. They can then be asked to repeat the experiment for themselves to see if they can obtain similar results and record their observations diagrammatically.

This demonstration or exercise would be more fruitful if children are provided with an opportunity prior to the demonstration and experiments to predict how they think the waves will behave. They should be asked to draw pictures and show what they think will happen in the following situations.

(*a*) In figure 6.3, discuss and then show on the diagram what will happen to the waves after hitting the barrier.

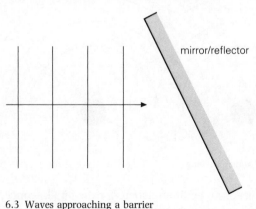

mirror/reflector

6.3 Waves approaching a barrier

(*b*) What will happen to the waves in figure 6.4 when they reach the shallow water where they travel more slowly?

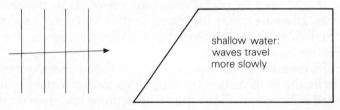

shallow water: waves travel more slowly

6.4 Waves approaching shallow water

(*c*) What will happen to the waves in figure 6.5 as they pass through the barrier?

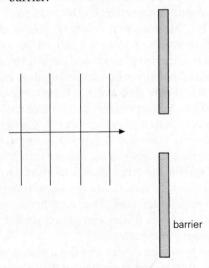

barrier

6.5 Waves approaching a narrow gap in a barrier

(*d*) What will happen where the two waves in figure 6.6 cross?

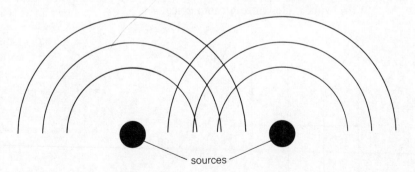

sources

6.6 Two circular waves crossing

These exercises will act as an additional focus for the pupils, concentrating their attention on specific aspects of the phenomenon. In addition it will provide a useful opportunity for them to explore any intuitive concepts that they may have about waves and contrast these with their observations. Any resulting conflict will provide a more fruitful learning opportunity. Even after this it would be naïve to expect the pupil diagrams to correspond with those presented in textbooks. These are merely the agreed symbolic representations of physicists and the teacher's role is to present these to children as a means of recording their observations.

When discussing the results of the experiments, various models are useful for explaining the observations. Reflection can be discussed in terms of tennis balls bouncing off walls, though the analogy is not a strong one. However it is one with which many pupils are familiar and is generally readily accepted. Refraction is best demonstrated outside with the pupils. Ask eight of them to link arms and to march forward in step. Now ask the rest of the class how this line could possibly turn a corner. The view should emerge that this is only possible if the pupils at one end slow down or practically stop. Now draw a line across the ground at an acute angle to the pupils and ask, those pupils who cross the line to slow down by taking half steps. This should have the same effect as that observed for the waves passing in shallow water. It generally also results in much hilarity and falling over, but if all pupils are provided with an opportunity to try this the point is made effectively and enjoyably.

Diffraction is a surprising phenomenon. It is easy to see that it is unlikely that a wave would simply penetrate through the gap in a linear fashion without affecting the adjacent water. Fortunately, there is a simple model of diffraction that explains the observed effect of the spreading of the wave on the other side of the gap or edge. When a plane wave meets a narrow gap, it causes the water in the gap to go up and down. The water does not know in what way this is different to a point source and a circular wave is sent out[9].

Various models are available for explaining what happens when two waves cross. The effect is known as *wave superposition* which results in a wave interference pattern. Some dramatic hand waving can be used to show that the effect of adding a 'flip-up' and a 'flip-down' would be nil (destructive interference) while adding a 'flip-up' and a 'flip-up' would result in a large 'flip-up' (constructive interference). This can also be shown convincingly by various computer programs that allow two waves and their sum to be displayed in an animated form[4], or by the use of two large plastic model waves. The latter are useful for demonstrating how the interference pattern emerges as a result of the waves arriving at a point taking different times to travel to that point (figure 6.7). Waves from source 2 that arrive at P in step with, or a whole number behind, those from source 1 will constructively interfere. Waves from source 2

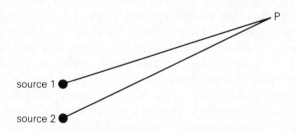

6.7 Different distances travelled by two waves from sources to point P

that arrive exactly out of step will destructively interfere and there will be no disturbance at this point. This is shown convincingly by a computer program called *Young's Slits*[10] which has the advantage of showing the waves between the sources and point P in an animated form. The point P can be moved graphically up and down the screen and the resultant combination of the two superposed waves is shown on the right-hand side of the screen. This is sufficient explanation of the phenomenon for most pupils. More able pupils will need to develop an understanding of the effect on the pattern of changing the source separation and the wavelength. The development of the full mathematical treatment is one approach to this and is necessary if the effect is to be used to determine the wavelength of light at A-level.

It is useful to show a wide variety of other waves interfering at this point to reinforce the concept of interference. Sound waves can be shown to interfere by attaching two small speakers in parallel to a signal generator and setting the frequency to approximately 100 Hz. This is best done outside where there are no spurious reflections, but is still effective indoors. Ask the pupils to move their heads from side to side. They should experience 'loud' and 'quiet' patches of sound. Then proceed by asking them to stand in a 'quiet' patch. With sufficient pupils the pattern of pupils that emerges bears a strong similarity to the pattern observed in the ripple tank. If the school has a 3 cm microwave apparatus, this can be used to demonstrate microwaves interfering. Finally it is useful to demonstrate interference from a light source. This is most easily done with a laser[11] as this is a bright, monochromatic[12] light source. Two lines are ruled on a microscope slide coated with Aquadag[13] with a needle approximately 0.1 mm apart and the beam from the laser passed through the slits. The waves diffract as the slits and then produce an interference pattern on the screen called interference fringes. This effect can only be explained in terms of the behaviour of waves and is evidence that light is a form of wave motion. The laser can also be used to show single slit diffraction effectively by passing the light through a narrow slit formed from two razor blades which are moved close together.

This provides a useful point to introduce the idea that light is part of a whole family of waves known as electromagnetic waves. Radio waves and microwaves may well have been introduced. Infra-red waves are normally demonstrated by placing a phototransistor beyond the red in a spectrum produced by a prism or a diffraction grating. This is not an easy or terribly convincing demonstration to perform and it is easier to start by asking pupils to place their warm hand a few millimetres from their face and ask how they are able to sense its presence. Placing a large metal parabolic mirror in front of the face has an even more dramatic effect. This can then proceed to the standard demonstration. Most home remote control units use infra-red diodes to transmit the pulses that control modern televisions and video recorders. They can be used to show the existence of a radiation which is invisible which reflects off objects. The remote control device still works when pointed directly away from the television and towards the opposite wall, as the radiation reflects off the wall.

Ultra-violet is best demonstrated by placing a piece of 'day-glo' material in a spectrum produced by a prism or diffraction grating. When compared with the spectrum on ordinary paper, there appears to be visible radiation beyond the marked position of the end of the blue. This is because the 'day-glo' material absorbs ultra-violet radiation and re-emits it in the visible spectrum. This explains why this material appears particularly bright and noticeable. Photocopy paper and many washing powders also contain ultra-violet fluorescers which perform the same function and explains the phrase 'whiter than white' commonly used by the advertisers of such products. Children are also fascinated by discussions of the effects of ultra-violet on themselves. Ultra-violet waves are the waves that cause tanning. However, despite the experience of physical well-being experienced from sitting in the sun, the radiation is energetic enough to damage the cells causing sunburn, skin cancer and damage to the lower layers of the epidermis which results in the tissue losing its elasticity in later years causing the skin to appear very wrinkled.

The full range of the electromagnetic spectrum is best discussed by the use of a chart[14,15]. The essential point to make is that this family of waves all have the same velocity and become more energetic as the wavelength diminishes and the frequency increases. This does not answer the question of what an electromagnetic wave is. This is because the wave does not travel through a physical medium like the surface of water or molecules of air. The best we can do is to point to the fact that mechanical waves consist of oscillating objects or particles in a medium. Electromagnetic waves are caused by oscillating electric charges. We cannot observe the e-m wave directly, only its many effects. It is simply a propagating disturbance in the electric and magnetic fields that exist throughout space. To appreciate this though requires some understanding of the concept of an electric field. This is something which is only introduced at A-level and it is much better to concentrate on the effects and uses of e-m waves and admit that we are not going to give pupils a full explanation.

Notes and references

1 Gilbert J.K. & Watts D.M. (1983) 'Concepts, misconceptions and alternative conceptions: Changing perspectives in science education.' *Studies in Science Education*, **10**, 61–98.
2 The video *Waves* is part of the Science Topics Series, BBC, 1984.
3 Brush, S.G. (1974) 'Should the history of science be rated X?' *Science*, **183**, 1164–72.
4 *Transverse Waves II*, Heinemann, London.
5 *Longitudinal Waves*, Heinemann, London.
6 See appendix 2 for details of the approach to mathematical manipulations necessary for this operation.
7 Driver R. (1983) *The Pupil as Scientist?* Open University Press, Milton Keynes.
8 For an effective demonstration of the phenomenon it is worth noting the following technical points with the apparatus. (*a*) Reflection is best demonstrated using a single pulse rather than a continuous train. (*b*) Refraction requires a glass plate which is *only just* covered with water for any noticeable deviation of the wave direction to occur. (*c*) Diffraction effects are most noticeable when the gap between the barriers is the same size as the wavelength. (*d*) Interference effects are generally most clearly seen by using continuous waves produced by two circular dippers about 30–40 mm apart.
9 A fuller explanation of the effects of diffraction is dependent on an idea known as 'Huygens Construction'. This in itself is an abstract idea and involves splitting the wavefront into an arbitrary number of secondary sources. It is effective at explaining the effects but it is not an idea that should be presented to children before A-level.
10 *Young's Slits*, Heinemann, London. This program is available for a BBC micro or a 380Z.
11 School lasers are quite safe providing no attempt is made to look directly up the beam. This can happen indirectly if the beam is reflected from a polished metal surface. For further advice teachers should refer to the DES memorandum 'The Use of Lasers in Schools.'
12 Lasers are unique amongst light sources in that they produce light of exactly one wavelength. Light produced by a normal light bulb is white light which

contains all the visible wavelengths. What makes lasers such effective sources for these demonstrations is that all the light waves are produced in step with each other. Such a source is said to be a 'coherent' source of light.

13 Aquadag is a graphite solution which is painted onto the slide and allowed to dry. And alternative to this is to purchase slides ready-made with the correct slit separation from the manufacturers.

14 Charts showing the electromagnetic spectrum are available from Pictorial Charts Educational Trust, 27 Kirchen Rd, London W13.

15 The series *Electricity in Industry* from the Electricity Council, 30 Millbank, London, SW1 4RD also has a chart showing the electromagnetic spectrum and its uses in industry.

7 Radioactivity and atomic structure

This topic often appears at the end of physics courses and is the nearest approach to modern physics. Most of the discoveries were made over the period 1890 to 1932 and gave birth to the fascinating developments of nuclear physics in the past 50 years which have substantially enhanced our understanding of matter. The ideas introduced are primarily descriptive and non-quantitative and generally appeal to pupils. The areas of difficulty for the pupil with these topics are the nature of random decay, the concept of half-life and the use of models. For the teacher problems arise with the units used for quantitative measurements of radioactivity, and the fact that it is difficult to find clear and relatively unbiased treatments of the nuclear power issue.

One reason why the physics of atomic structure is difficult to understand is that atoms are unimaginably small and cannot be seen. All the evidence we have about what atoms are like is indirect and we construct mental models to explain our observations. Pupils are asked to make quite bold steps from experimental evidence to the inferences and hypotheses that are currently accepted. In addition, much of the experimental evidence is not demonstrable in the school science laboratory, putting the pupil (and the teacher) at one further remove from reality. On the other hand, radioactivity is a phenomenon that allows physics students to be aware of individual atoms, as they decay a click is heard from the counter.

Historical approach

In developing models of the atom most teachers use a historical approach. The key experiment that led to the development of the modern picture of atomic structure was done by Geiger and Marsden in 1913, working under Rutherford. They fired alpha particles towards a thin gold foil in a vacuum. At that time there was no clear idea about what atoms were like inside. From other experiments, however, alpha particles were already known to be helium nuclei, and therefore smaller than atoms; atoms were known to be made up of other sub-particles; and atoms in solids were known to be packed closely together.

Various models for the structure of atoms had been proposed, for example, the 'solid ball' model and the 'plum pudding' model (figure 7.1). Pupils can be asked to exercise their own imagination and to propose a structure for atoms. What do they imagine an atom would look like? Pupils should then be asked to predict the result of the Geiger–Marsden experiment with their postulated atomic structures.

Finally, pupils can be presented with the results that Geiger and Marsden

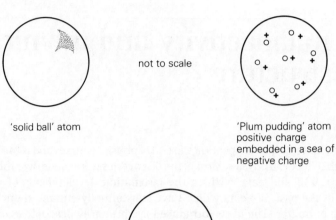

'solid ball' atom

'Plum pudding' atom
positive charge
embedded in a sea of
negative charge

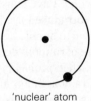

'nuclear' atom

7.1 Some models of atomic structure

obtained. Almost all of the alpha particles passed straight through, with the few that were deflected being deflected through large angles. A very few (1 in 10 000) were scattered back from the metal foil. This was very surprising as it was known that the alpha particles were relatively massive and moved with a velocity of about 10% of the velocity of light. Rutherford used a potent metaphor: that the result was as surprising as if a 15 inch (about 40 cm) diameter cannon shell had been fired at a piece of tissue paper and it had bounced back.

With this preparation, during discussion pupils can be led to deduce much of the relevant details of the structure of the atom; that is, almost all of an atom is empty space, and there is a small massive object in the centre of atoms that can deflect alpha particles through large angles because it is substantially more massive than the alpha particle and has a large positive electrostatic charge. This positive charge repels the incident alpha particle scattering it in a new direction.

There are a number of aids to understanding this result. One is the use of computer models, for example, *Alpha Scattering*[1]. It is also valuable to demonstrate a model consisting of a one-dimensional array of pins stuck in a board (figure 7.2). The pins are covered with tissue paper and marbles thrown at them. The pupils are then asked to infer from the scattering what kind of object the marbles must be hitting.

It is useful to have some analogies for sizes available.

The nucleus of most atoms is about 1/10 000 of the size of the whole atom. If the nucleus of an atom is represented by a pinhead 1 mm in radius, the whole atom would be 10 m across!

If a nucleus was the same size as a tennis ball, then the electrons would be about 1 km away.

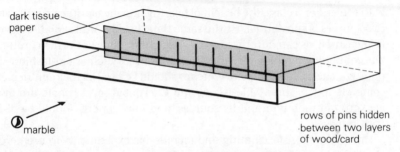

dark tissue paper

marble

rows of pins hidden between two layers of wood/card

7.2 Two-dimensional analogy of the Geiger–Marsden experiment

If an atom was the size of Wembley stadium, then the nucleus would be the size of a pea, and the electrons would be like mosquitos flying round the edge.

If they could be packed closely together, all the nuclei in your body could be packed into a single grain of sand.

A neutron star is made of collapsed atoms, and has a density of 10 000 000 kg/cm³.

These numbers will surprise almost all pupils!

Radiation and decay

Most physics courses to GCSE attempt to cover three themes in this topic in the following order: (i) the detection and properties of ionising radiation, (ii) the nature of radioactive decay and (iii) the model of the atom.

Use of the term 'ionising radiation' often causes confusion. Ionising radiation is, of course, simply radiation that can cause ionisation. This means that each quantum of radiation, or particle, has at least sufficient energy to break covalent chemical bonds in some medium. The medium usually being considered is living tissue, and the relevant chemical bonds are in the cell proteins and the nucleic acids responsible for heredity. Alpha particles are very highly ionising, and beta particles (electrons) and gamma radiation are less so. Alpha particles can generate several thousand ion pairs ('break several thousand bonds') in each millimetre of their travel. By contrast, ultra-violet light quanta usually have only enough energy to break one bond, and microwave radiation quanta have insufficient energy to break chemical bonds at all. The energy carried by microwave radiation is absorbed in the chemical bonds increasing the vibrational energy of the molecules and warming the material; this is the principle of microwave ovens.

Practical work in radioactivity can be undertaken according to the DES Administrative Memorandum[2]. Many Local Education Authorities have their own safety regulations in addition to the DES regulations. All secondary schools which possess radioactive sources should have a Radiation Protection Supervisor, who is usually the Head of the Science (or Physics) Department. Most secondary schools have a standard set of radioactive sources and apparatus which must be kept in a locked cupboard. The only approved sources are sealed and are very weak indeed. They pose no heath risk if handled properly with tongs. For a class, the benefit of hearing and measuring a count rate from real sources is substantial. At the same time, background radiation levels can be measured, as can natural sources of radiation, such as Cornish granite, rock kits containing pitchblende, and artificial sources such as old-fashioned luminous watches. Only complete watches should be used as the radium paint can come off. Since Three Mile Island and Chernobyl most people are aware of background radiation and its sources, and implications should be discussed with pupils.

One of the most fascinating and memorable experiments to use here is the cloud chamber. The simplest and most effective one uses solid carbon dioxide to supercool ethanol vapour introduced on the surrounding felt (figure 7.3). This

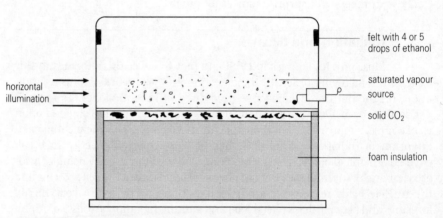

7.3 Cloud chamber

produces a supersaturated vapour cloud which will condense on any available site. The sites are provided by the ions produced by the alpha radiation from the weak source. Alpha radiation is intensely ionising producing typically a 100 000 ion pairs per centimetre. The resulting vapour trail can be clearly seen from above when the chamber is illuminated from the side. Rubbing the top with a duster to charge it electrostatically makes the chamber work more effectively. The incessant multitude of tracks gives a successful, clear picture of the radiation from a source. It also makes a useful assessment task in observation, as careful investigation should show tracks of different lengths corresponding to alpha particles of different energies, tracks where collisions have clearly occurred because of the sudden divergence from their previous path, and some tracks which are not linear but more random and fainter which are produced by beta particles.

One problem with this apparatus is obtaining a supply of solid carbon dioxide. This is normally produced by expanding compressed carbon dioxide through a small aperture. The apparatus is available from commercial apparatus suppliers and most fire extinguisher firms will replenish the cylinders.

It is straightforward and rewarding to repeat Bequerel's experiment to demonstrate that some materials emit radiation that can pass through light-proof paper and still expose photographic film. With school sources overnight exposure is necessary, followed by overdeveloping.

Random decay

The nature of random decay and of half-life are best approached through games and simulations. For example, take around 100 dice and throw them. This can be done quite easily in a class of 25, each pupil with four dice. The dice marked with a six are deemed to have decayed, and are removed. The remainder are thrown again, with every die showing a six being removed. A graph like that in figure 7.4 will be obtained. Roughly one sixth of all the dice

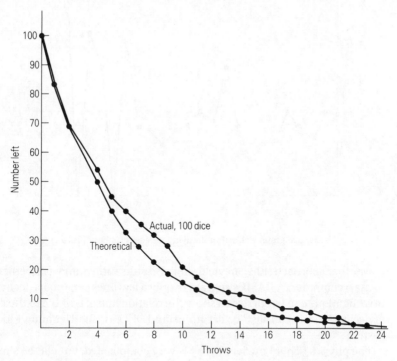

7.4 Graph of number remaining against throw

remaining will decay each time the dice are thrown. The outcome for a particular die, which may be marked at the start, is completely unpredictable. The half-life for this system is roughly four throws, that is, whatever number of dice that you start with, it takes about four throws for half of them to have come up six. This can form the basis of an extended class activity. For example, pupils can investigate the outcome of removing other numbers than six, odd numbers, or numbers less than five.

Another feature of this model that reflects reality is that the decay rate, that is, the number of dice decaying per throw, is proportional to the number of dice left. Of course, since there are far fewer dice in the model than even the smallest available radioactive source, the random fluctuations are proportionally greater. This facet of radioactive decay can be illuminated by drawing a graph of the fraction of the dice decaying each turn against the number of dice remaining. When the number of a dice is large, the fraction decaying is close to the predicted 0.166 ($\frac{1}{6}$). As the number of dice decreases, the random fluctuations increase in amplitude (figure 7.5).

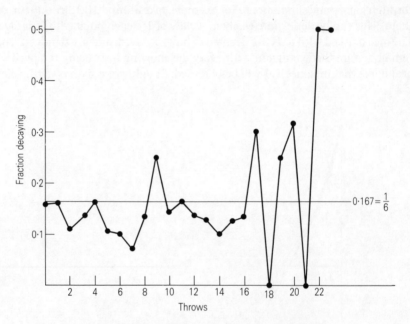

7.5 Typical graph of fraction decaying against number of throws

Another approach that can yield similar results rather more conveniently, is to use a computer. A BASIC program of only a few lines can model decay well[3]. Investigations can be carried to show the relationship of half-life to the chance of decay. Models can also be set up using LOGO, or the Dynamic Modelling System.

The physics behind nuclear decay is very complicated, but can be simplified by explaining that the larger the nucleus the less stable it is. A somewhat messy (literally) analogy that can be used here involves plastic bags or balloons with water in. As more water is added the 'nucleus' becomes increasingly unstable, finally bursting. The stability of the nucleus is dependent on the neutron/proton balance. There is no simple explanation for the importance of this and most pupils are prepared to take it on trust that atomic nuclei decay so as roughly to maintain the proton/neutron balance. Connecting a Geiger–Muller counter to a loudspeaker provides an audible demonstration of decay. Pupils can become quite fascinated by the fact that they are listening to individual atoms breaking up.

Applications of radioactivity include radioactive tracing, food irradiation, the destruction of carcinogenic tissue and radiocarbon dating. If doctors wish to check the functioning of a specific organ, one technique they can use is to inject some soluble radioactive isotope into the bloodstream. The material is absorbed by the organ under study and the radioactivity in the patient's body is mapped using a device known as a gamma camera. The picture constructed shows the size of the organ and how efficiently it is absorbing the material. The tracer has a short half-life so that the radioactivity diminishes rapidly over a few hours.

Carbon dating makes use of the isotope carbon-14 which has a half-life of 5730 years. An equilibrium concentration of carbon-14 exists in the atmosphere because the rate of decay is matched by the production of carbon-14 by the action of cosmic rays on nitrogen-14 nuclei. Living plants use carbon dioxide in the atmosphere for photosynthesis. When they die the carbon-14 slowly decays and is not replaced. Carbon-containing objects can be dated back as much as 10 000 years using this method. A computer package[4] has been written to make these concepts accessible to junior secondary pupils. Videos demonstrating applications of radioactivity are easily available from the UKAEA[5] and the BBC[6].

Radioactivity units

This section is included in this book as the new system of units has not yet reached all the textbooks in schools. *Living with radiation* from the National Radiological Protection Board[7] gives a clear and more extensive study of units and issues than can be attempted here.

The activity of a source is now measured in a unit called the becquerel, symbol Bq. A source of 1 Bq has a disintegration rate of 1 nucleus per second. The sources used in schools may have activities of around 10 000 Bq. One gram of plutonium-239 has an activity of 2000 MBq (2×10^9 Bq). The old system of units based on the curie, symbol Ci, is still widely used and many school sources are labelled in microcuries, symbol μCi. To convert from μCi to Bq, multiply by 3×10^4.

The half-life of a source is given in units of time suitable to the period. It may be given in seconds, minutes, or years.

The absorbed dose is measured in a unit called the gray, symbol Gy. It is a measure of the energy transferred to one kilogram of matter. One gray corresponds to one joule per kilogram. Since the types of radiation cause varying degrees of harm, a further measure is used, the dose equivalent, expressed in a unit called the sievert, symbol Sv. For gamma rays, beta particles (electrons) and X-rays, the dose equivalent is the same as the absorbed dose. Alpha particles are much more likely to cause harm for the same dose, so the absorbed dose is multiplied by 20 to give the dose equivalent. It is initially surprising that alpha radiation which cannot pass through a single sheet of paper has a much higher dose equivalent than beta radiation or gamma radiation. The reason for the extra dose equivalent for alpha radiation is because alpha particles have a very short range, any particle that contains alpha emitters that becomes lodged in the lung, for instance, gives a very high dose to the volume of lung immediately surrounding the particle. The most feared material in this respect is plutonium. Plutonium oxide particles are highly insoluble and, once lodged firmly in the small passages in the lung, the body's natural mechanisms cannot remove them.

Nuclear power

In an age when the generation of electricity by nuclear power is one of the most important applications of science that arouses strong debate, it is important to give pupils a clear understanding of the process. There are two contexts within which physics teachers ought to operate. First, the science and technology of the operation of nuclear power stations, and second, the range of issues, whether technological, economic, ethical or moral as to the rights and wrongs of nuclear power. Details of the former can be found in any standard text. There are several basic primers to the issues involved in nuclear power[8,9]. The first reference in particular gives a clear introduction to the terms and jargon used in the debate. There is a large body of literature for the anti-nuclear case produced by groups such as Greenpeace[10], Friends of the Earth[11], and the Centre for Alternative Technology[12]. A large number of videos, slides and printed materials on nuclear energy and radioactivity are produced by the Education Departments of the UKAEA and the CEGB, and distributed by the Electricity Council[13].

Nuclear power generation raises a number of important issues such as the siting of the power stations, the storage and transportation of waste and threats to civil liberties. Nearly all of these involve the assessment of what is an acceptable risk. The actual dangers from ionising radiation are calculated from the calculated or measured total dose to the whole population. The NRPB gives a pie chart[7] for the total dose received by people in the UK (figure 7.6). This shows that, averaged over the whole population, only about 22% of the dose equivalent is received from artificial sources, and of that 22%, over 20% is from medical sources such as X-rays. The total averaged dose is about 2400 μSv/year. Of course, this varies greatly depending on where you live and what you do, but is seems to be generally accepted that the average death rate will not be affected by changes in this distribution.

The overall risk factor for cancer is about 1.25×10^{-2}/Sv. That is, if a population of 80 people is given a dose of 1 Sv each, then one of those people is likely to develop a cancer. Assuming a population of 50 000 000 and an average dose of 2400 μSv year^{-1}, then about 1500 people each year will develop radiation-induced cancer. Of this number, 32 or so could have been prevented by avoiding all medical dosage, and about two could have been avoided by total abstinence from nuclear power and nuclear bomb tests.

This could be compared with, for instance, numbers dying on the roads, in mines, from smoking, or from any other cause. What is it that makes one risk acceptable rather than another?

What about accidental doses? The accidents at Windscale, Three Mile Island and Chernobyl cause considerable concern. The total amount and type of

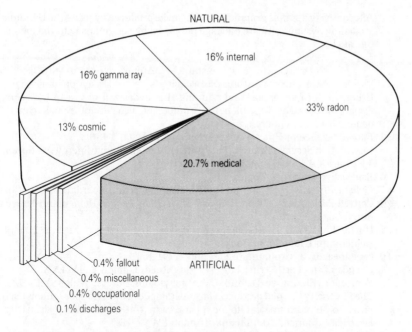

NATURAL

16% internal

16% gamma ray

33% radon

13% cosmic

20.7% medical

0.4% fallout   ARTIFICIAL
0.4% miscellaneous
0.4% occupational
0.1% discharges

7.6 Average annual radiation dose for population of the UK

radioactive material released in each of these accidents has been more or less closely determined, and various long-term fatality figures have been calculated. These vary from small numbers, of the order of 10, of fatalities from Windscale and Three Mile Island, and of the order of hundreds or thousands from Chernobyl.

This whole issue is a prime example of the entitlement of future citizens to factual information and the intellectual tools to use it sensibly as part of a democracy. Our duty as science teachers is to provide this basic entitlement without allowing ourselves to slip into persuasion and rhetoric, on either side. Students should be exposed to the arguments on both sides and allowed to form their own judgements after critical review of the evidence. Role-play exercises are particularly valuable here and the SATIS materials[14] provide an excellent exercise on siting a nuclear power station.

Notes and references

1 *Alpha Scattering*, Computers in the Curriculum, Longmans.
2 DES Administrative Memorandum on Radioactivity, HMSO, London.
3 The following is a short BASIC program which will simulate the throwing of 100 dice printing the number of atoms remaining at each throw:

```
10 LET NOATOMS = 100
20 LET DECAYCONSTANT = 1/6
30 PRINT "THROW", "NO OF ATOMS REMAINING"
40 FOR THROW = 1 TO 6
50 NODECAYING = DECAYCONSTANT * NOATOMS
60 NOATOMS = NOATOMS-NODECAYING
70 PRINT NOATOMS THROW
80 NEXT THROW
```

Alternatively a simple graphical model can be produced by using the Dynamic Modelling System software package published by Longmans with the following model.

Model	*Values*
NoDecaying = DecayConstant * NoAtoms	NoAtoms = 100
NoAtoms = NoAtoms-NoDecaying	DecayConstant = 1/6

Using the 'Graph' option and running the model will give a quick visual display of the way in which the number of dice 'decay' which can be demonstrated to children.

4 *Dating*, Science in Process Software, Capital Media, 1986.
5 Information Services Branch, The United Kingdom Atomic Energy Authority, 11 Charles II Street, London SW1Y 4YW.
6 *Radioactivity*, Science Topics, BBC.
7 *Living with radiation*, National Radiological Protection Board, HMSO, 1986.
8 Cottrell FRS., Alan (1981) *How Safe is Nuclear Energy?*, Heinemann Educational Books.
9 Hoyle, Fred (1979) *Energy or Extinction: The Case for Nuclear Energy*, Heinemann Educational Books.
10 Greenpeace, 36 Graham Street, London N1 8LL.
11 Friends of the Earth Trust Ltd, 377 City Road, London EC1V 1NA.
12 Centre for Alternative Technology, Machynlleth, Powys, Wales SY20 9AZ.
13 The Electricity Council produce a large catalogue of materials for schools each year. To obtain a free catalogue, please write to Understanding Electricity, Electricity Council, 30 Millbank, London SW1P 4RD.
14 Science and Technology in Society (SATIS), Association for Science Education, 1986.

8 Basic electronics

The inclusion of electronics in modern science syllabuses has caused problems for many physics teachers let alone non-specialists. Yet before condemning the topic as an ephemeral fashion it is worth asking how many teachers can recall such items as Searles' bar, Fletcher's trolley or the Wimshurst machine. These were all in regular use in the teaching of physics in the 1950s and are now collectors' items. Science teaching is in part a reflection of the technology of the time and the curriculum responds to the needs of society. The prevalence of electronic systems in modern society demands that pupils are provided with some insight into this important technology at school. Responsibility for this often falls on the science teacher. There has been a substantial debate[1] regarding the place of electronics within physics. Electronics is a hybrid subject in that many of the principles of the devices are explained by physics, while the construction and application of the circuits involves skills of design, construction and communication that are often thought to be more relevant to the CDT department. A broader view is proposed by Black & Harrison[2] who see technology as a human endeavour that calls on human resources, skill and natural phenomena to satisfy human needs. Electronics and the underlying physics is just one more resource that we can use to solve human problems. The emphasis on electronics is due to the fact that many solutions to human problems do incorporate an electronic device. Many simple circuits can be seen by children to be immediately relevant in fulfilling human needs and this helps to make it a subject of great motivation.

For the non-specialist, there is some reassurance in that a recent study identified this topic as an area which non-physicists anticipated would cause them difficulties. In practice, less than 20% reported electronics to be an area of difficulty. The fundamental argument in electronics teaching in recent years has been between those who advocate a 'systems' approach and those who prefer to approach the subject through circuit construction from discrete components. In the systems approach, electronic devices are seen as an assembly of sub-units each of which performs a specific function. An outline of a digital watch is shown in figure 8.1. At its simplest, this system can be thought of as consisting of four units (blocks of electronic components): one unit, the crystal oscillator, provides a fixed frequency train of pulses; another unit divides the pulses so that there is one pulse per second, one per minute, and so on, which is used to count the seconds and minutes; the third unit is a display unit which interprets the binary numbers and is able to display them in decimal; and the final unit allows the clock to be set and reset to whatever time is appropriate. All that is necessary then to construct our digital watch is to find

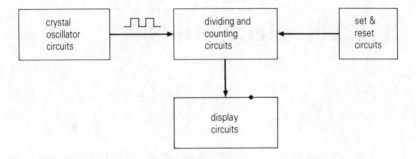

8.1 System diagram of a digital watch

circuits which perform these functions, and connect them together appropriately. Such units are the building blocks of many electronic devices and are
commonly available. The emphasis is on what function the circuit performs,
rather than how it works. This has lead to manufacturers producing kits[3] with
boards that perform specific processes. Building an electronic system then
becomes a process of analysing the problem, selecting the appropriate sub-
units and connecting them together to perform the necessary function. In the
case of the digital watch, it is possible to purchase one chip which performs all
the operations outlined above.

The argument behind this approach is that integration of circuits has meant
that only the chip designers need to know the complex detail of assembling
individual components to build a specific circuit. The designers of electronic
artefacts need to understand how to assemble these integrated circuits to build
the electronic systems they require. Nearly all GCSE syllabuses have now
moved to the systems approach and this is recommended to the non-specialist
who does not appreciate the finer complexities of electronic circuits and
components. A pupil who is shown the nature of these 'electronic building
blocks' and gains an appreciation of their function and inter-relationships will
have a more useful knowledge than one who has spent weeks learning the
intricacies of one or two circuits.

In addition, most of the 'systems' approach can be taught more readily
through the use of kits which obviate the need for soldering or other problematic methods of construction, such as breadboards. For many teachers this will
be a great relief and has the advantage that the basic concepts of the subject can
be covered more rapidly. Finally, many of these kits are supported by materials
designed for pupils and teachers and are often written with the non-specialist in
mind[4].

Using discrete components for the teaching of electronics can only be
recommended to teachers who feel confident with the constructional methods.
In addition, a substantial investment of time and effort is often necessary to
correct the pupil's inevitable errors and ensure success. The main advantage is
that it requires less of an initial investment in equipment. However, the
running costs are higher and, if soldering is being used, low voltage soldering
irons will have to be purchased. There is a substantial risk of pupils burning
through the cable and electrocuting themselves with mains soldering irons.

100

Basic concepts in electronics

The basic concept of electronic systems can be summarised very simply by figure 8.2. A course by Geddes[5] makes this an essential feature. Most

8.2 Basic concept of electronic systems

physics courses require a study of some of the devices that perform the central operation of processing the input, such as the transistor and logic gates. Variable resistance devices (like the thermistor, and light-dependent resistor) are then examined as devices for sensing changes and producing inputs which are processed and output to loudspeakers, light-emitting diodes (LED) and relays.

Process devices

A pure systems approach would treat all the process devices as black boxes which perform specific functions. The process they perform on a given input is all that the pupil has to learn. However, natural curiosity demands a fuller explanation if possible. The single transistor switch is explicable in terms of simple models which are comprehensible to the average pupil.

The single transistor switch

Many models have been devised to show the nature of the transistor and its behaviour. One of the simplest is the analogy of a valve-controlled pipeline (figure 8.3). The current in the main pipeline, that is from collector to emitter, is controlled by the much smaller current in the small pipeline, that is from base to emitter. If there is no current from the base to the emitter, the valve A is closed and no current can flow through the main pipeline. However if more than 0.7 V is applied across the base–emitter junction, the valve A is opened and a large current flows between the collector and the emitter. Hence the transistor is a two-state device which is either 'on' or 'off'. The real transistor does not actually contain a valve but the model provides a useful concrete illustration.

Another excellent model of the transistor as a valve-controlled gate is shown in a poster from Pictorial Charts[6] (figure 8.4). Here a few of the electrons are piped through the base–emitter junction. In passing through the small gate they automatically open the main gate of the collector–emitter junction. This shows that the collector–emitter current is controlled by the base–emitter current. This model is perhaps even more effective when talking about field effect transistors (FETS) which have largely replaced the bipolar type pre-

101

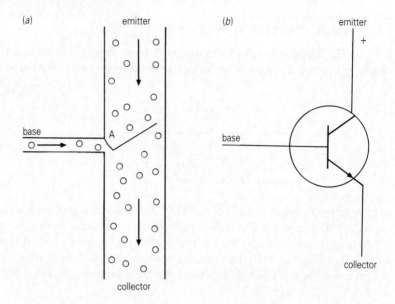

8.3 Water analogy and symbol for the transistor

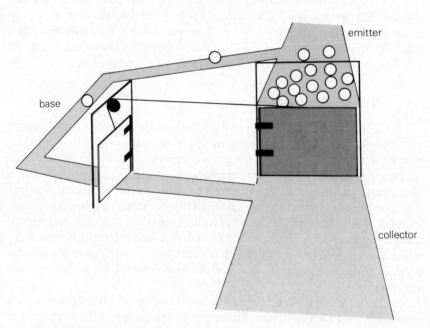

8.4 Model of the behaviour of a transistor

viously outlined. The terminals of these are known as source, gate and drain. The gate is the electrode which controls the flow of current from source to drain.

The state of the transistor is readily shown by placing a bulb in the collector–emitter circuit as shown in the circuit in figure 8.5. The 1 kΩ resistor in the base circuit is essential to prevent too much current flowing between the base

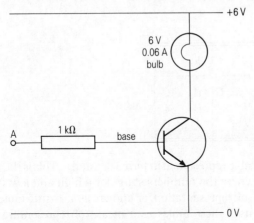

8.5 Simple transistor circuit containing a bulb

and the emitter and overheating the transistor. Joining point A to 6 V should turn the light on and touching it to 0 V will turn it off. This circuit is able to sense the state of the input A and change state accordingly. This means it *processes* the input.

Logic gates

(a) *The NOT gate.* The simplest logic gate is made by attaching an extra wire at C to the circuit in figure 8.6. C is now the output of the circuit whose

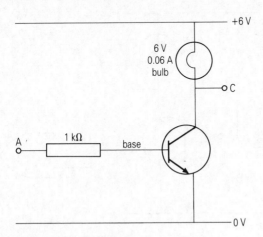

8.6 Transistor-based NOT gate

state is measured by attaching a voltmeter between C and 0 V. Joining point A to + 6 V turns 'on' the transistor, causing point C to drop to a potential ≈ 0 V.

103

This is because nearly all the potential is dropped across the lamp as it drives the current through it. The output is now NOT the input and therefore this is known as a NOT gate. This can be represented as in table 8.1.

Table 8.1

(a)		(b)	
Input A	Output C	A	C
0 V	6 V	0	1
6 V	0 V	1	0

Table 8.1 (b) shows the table represented in terms of 1 and 0. This is the normal form of representation where the numbers stand for a high and low voltages respectively. This form of representation is known as a 'truth table', after Wiggenstein who first used these tables as a means of representing logical statements. The circuit performs a basic logical operation on the input. The standard symbol for a NOT gate is shown in figure 8.7.

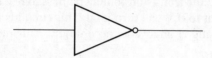

8.7 NOT gate symbol

(b) *The NOR gate.* The circuit can be extended to make a NOR gate, that is, one whose output is only high when neither one input NOR the other is high, by adding an extra lead and 1 kΩ resistor to the base as shown in figure 8.8. There

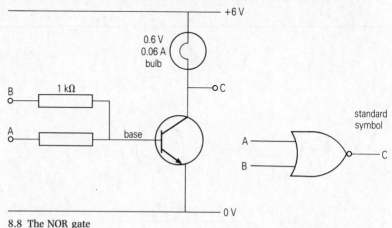

8.8 The NOR gate

are now four possible combinations of inputs on A and B which give the outputs shown in column C in table 8.2 (a). Table 8.2(b) shows this is reduced to a truth table.

104

Table 8.2

(a)			(b)		
A	B	C	A	B	C
0 V	0 V	6 V	0	0	1
0 V	6 V	0 V	0	1	0
6 V	0 V	0 V	1	0	0
6 V	6 V	0 V	1	1	0

(c) *The OR gate.* This is the inverse of the NOR gate. So while columns A and B are always the same for any gate, as they represent all possible combinations of two inputs, column C will be the exact opposite of that in table 8.2 (see table 8.3).

Table 8.3

A	B	C
0	0	0
0	1	1
1	0	1
1	1	1

The logic of this gate is that the output is high when one input OR the other is high. Since it is the inverse of the NOR gate, the simplest way to construct it is to invert the output of a NOR gate, so that C is the NOT of a NOR gate. The only difference is that this symbol does not have a small circle on the output (figure 8.9). The small circle indicates that the output has been logically negated.

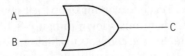

8.9 The OR gate

(d) *The AND gate.* The logic of an AND gate is that the output is only high when one input AND the other are high. Hence the 'truth table' would read as in table 8.4. The standard symbol for this is shown in figure 8.10.

Table 8.4

A	B	C
0	0	0
0	1	0
1	0	0
1	1	1

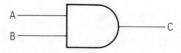

8.10 The AND gate

(e) *The NAND gate.* This, as its name implies, is NOT an AND gate. Hence the output is only high when one input AND the other are NOT high. The result is that the table for this is the inverse of that for the AND gate (see table 8.5). Again the small circle on the output shows that the output has been negated, (figure 8.11).

Table 8.5

A	B	C
0	0	1
0	1	1
1	0	1
1	1	0

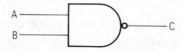

8.11 The NAND gate

All the kits marketed for teaching the subject contain boards which clearly illustrate the behaviour of these gates. Teachers can make up their own large-scale models with switches using the diagrams shown in figure 8.12. Such models make a good method of introducing the concepts to children. Given the circuits in figure 8.12, they can be demonstrated individually to pupils who can be asked to write down a sentence expressing the condition of the switches for the lamps to be 'on'. The electronics 11–13 kit and its associated book[7] takes just such an approach introducing logic operations using switches based on relays. The *Microelectronics for All* kit is the other very popular introduction. This makes use of just three gates, the NOT, AND and OR gates. The pupils combine these to make all the standard gates, but the approach is to allow the pupils an opportunity to explore the devices in a context of real problems, for example design a system that will turn the central heating on when it is dark and the temperature is too low. In addition, this kit is supplemented by an attractive set of workcards which allow the pupils to work through at their own rate. Other approaches using discrete components are not recommended as the point often gets lost in confusion generated by systems not working due to poor or wrong connections.

106

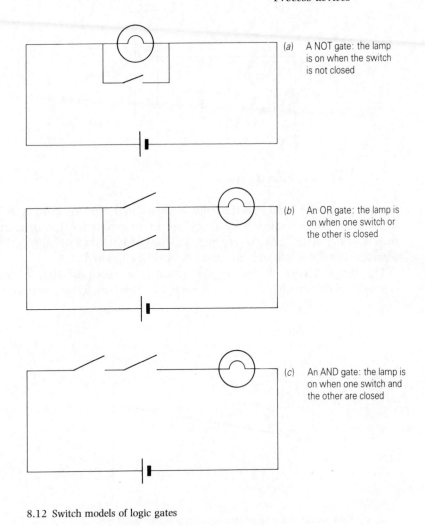

(a) A NOT gate: the lamp is on when the switch is not closed

(b) An OR gate: the lamp is on when one switch or the other is closed

(c) An AND gate: the lamp is on when one switch and the other are closed

8.12 Switch models of logic gates

The operational amplifier

This particular device has acquired something of a mystique. Essentially it is a small-scale integrated circuit which acts as a high gain amplifier. The term high gain implies that the output voltage is many times greater than the input voltage, typically 100 000. There are two inputs, an inverting input, labelled '$-$', where the output is always in the opposite sense to the input, that is if the input is positive the output is negative, and a normal non-inverting input labelled '$+$' (figure 8.13). However it would be wrong to refer to these inputs as the positive and negative inputs as both inputs can accept positive and negative voltages. The voltage output of the device is given by

$$V_{\text{out}} = A(V_2 - V_1)$$

where A is the gain of the amplifier, V_2 is the voltage applied to the non-

Basic electronics

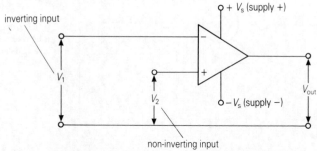

8.13 The operational amplifier

inverting input (+) and V_1 is the voltage applied to the inverting input (−). In addition the device is said to have a very high input impedance. This means that the resistance of the device is very high and the current that flows into the input terminal is very small and can nearly always be ignored.

The simplest way of viewing the device is to recognise that it can be represented by a model of a lever (figure 8.14). Here small movements on the

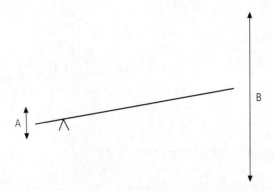

8.14 Model of the behaviour of the operational amplifier

left-hand side (A) create very large movements on the right-hand side (B). However, operational amplifiers are not normally used to produce large voltage gains. If used in this mode, the amplification is uneven across the frequency range. It is normal to limit the amplification of the device by applying negative feedback and feeding back some of the output voltage which is in the opposite sense to the input voltage. This is done by connecting a feedback resistor R_f from the output to the input as in figure 8.15. In all of these simple applications of the operational amplifier the non-inverting input is held at zero volts by connecting it to the 0 V rail. In addition there is normally an input resistor R_{in} which limits the input current and prevents damage to the amplifier.

It is now possible to derive a value for the amplification. This is done by assuming that the input voltage is practically zero and that there is no input current. Because the device has a very high input impedance (a.c. resistance). The circuit is rearranged diagramatically as shown in figure 8.16.

108

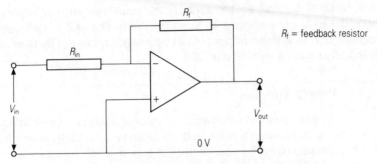

8.15 Simple circuit for the operational amplifier with negative feedback

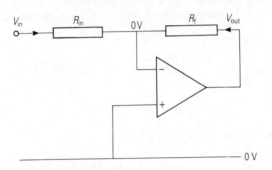

8.16 Alternative version of figure 8.15

The situation then is that the current through the input resistor is given by applying the relationship $I = V \div R$.

$$I = \frac{V_{in} - 0}{R_{in}}$$

and the current through the feedback resistor is

$$I = \frac{0 - V_{out}}{R_{out}}$$

Since no current flows into the amplifier, the value of the current is identical and equating these two gives

$$\frac{-V_{out}}{R_{out}} = \frac{V_{in}}{R_{in}}$$

or more commonly

$$\frac{-V_{out}}{V_{in}} = \frac{R_{out}}{R_{in}}$$

What this shows is that the size of the gain obtained with feedback is dependent on the ratio of the feedback resistance to the input resistance. By adjusting the ratio, the gain obtained can be carefully controlled and is independent of frequency, so all voltages are amplified by the same amount. This is an essential characteristic for a reliable amplifier.

Power supplies

All electronic devices require an electrical power supply. In nearly all cases this has to be a constant d.c. voltage. However, electricity is distributed by an alternating voltage system as this allows it to be transformed to high voltages which reduces transmission losses. Consequently it has to be converted to d.c. Most physics syllabuses require that the method of achieving this is understood by the pupils. The simplest block outline of the system is shown in figure 8.17.

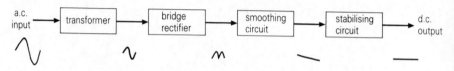

8.17 Block outline of power supply

The mains voltage is normally transformed from 240 V to an appropriate lower voltage by the use of a transformer. This alternating voltage then has to be converted to a d.c. voltage. The simplest method is to employ a diode, which is a one-way valve. This is not a very effective method of achieving a d.c. supply as current can only flow for half the time. The 50 Hz mains changes direction 100 times a second, so every alternate 1/100th second there will be no current. This is shown in figure 8.18.

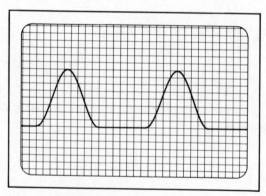

8.18 Rectified alternating current

To solve this problem, the bridge rectifier was invented. It simply uses four diodes in a rather clever combination so that the a.c. current is converted to a d.c. current for all the cycles of operation (figure 8.19). When A is positive, current will flow towards C through diode 1, round the external circuit and

110

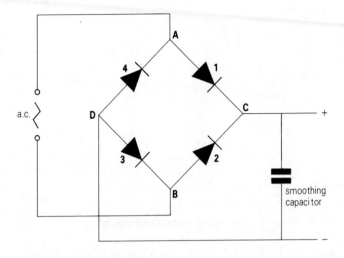

8.19 The bridge rectifier

back to B. When B is positive, current will again flow towards C through diode 2, around the external circuit and back to A. Hence, while the current in the external circuit can change direction, the current always flows in the same direction between C and D. This is very well illustrated by using light-emitting diodes for the diodes and a light-emitting diode with a 220 Ω resistor connected across C and D. The a.c. is provided by a slow a.c. generator. The current in the one diode is seen to flow in the same direction all the time as this diode remains continually on. The current in the bridge arrangement is observed to go first through one pair (1) and (3) and then the next pair (2) and (4) and so on. This arrangement is known as a bridge rectifier.

This is not the complete picture because even though the voltage is now only acting in one direction, the voltage varies between 0 and its maximum voltage, typically of the order of 10 to 20 V. This can be seen by connecting an oscilloscope to C and D. This is not satisfactory for running electronic circuits as these require a constant d.c. voltage and is achieved most simply by connecting a large capacitor across the output of the bridge rectifier. The capacitor acts as a large reservoir which fills with charge when the voltage is high. When the supply voltage drops, the charged capacitor sustains the voltage and the supply of electric charge to the circuit. A similar model is provided by the natural gas distribution network. The old gasometers are used as local stores of gas which are topped up when the drain from local demand is low. When the demand is high, the gasometer supplements the main supply. Figure 8.20 shows an equivalent model based on a water model and balloon. When the pressure drops, the balloon maintains the pressure and the supply of water. When the pressure at the supply rises, it fills the balloon with more water. In this way, variations in supply pressure are smoothed out.

The final component necessary in the circuit is a voltage stabiliser which, despite variations in the supply voltage or current drawn by the load, keeps the voltage supplied to the load constant. This is normally done using a component

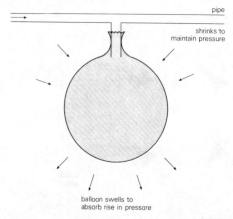

8.20 Water model of the effect of a smoothing capacitor

called a Zener diode. Normal diodes are one-way valves, they only allow current to flow in the direction indicated by the arrow on the symbol. Zener diodes will allow current to flow in the reverse direction when a certain voltage is exceeded. This is known as the 'breakdown voltage'. The Zener diode is normally included after the capacitor in an arrangement shown in figure 8.21.

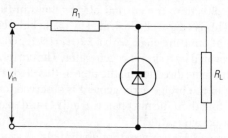

8.21 Zener diode stabilising circuit

R_L is the load resistor which determines the current drawn from the supply by the device. If the voltage at the input to this part of the circuit increases, more current flows through the diode in the reverse direction and the potential drop across R_1 is larger, which returns the voltage to its previous value. If the voltage at the input drops, less current flows through R_1 and the voltage drop across this resistor is less, keeping the voltage at its previous level. In this way the voltage is said to be stabilised and resistant to fluctuations in the current drawn by the circuit and voltage variations in the supply.

For much of the classroom experimental work, it is simpler to achieve a steady d.c. voltage using batteries. This has the advantage that much of the experimental work can be done in a room that is not fitted with a large number of mains sockets, particularly if kits are used that do not require soldering irons.

Conceptual difficulties in electronics

There are two main conceptual difficulties encountered in the teaching of electronics: pupils' inadequate models of the behaviour of electric currents, and a lack of understanding of the concept of voltage[8]. A circuit known as a 'potential divider', which is commonly used in electronics, illustrates both of these problems (figure 8.22). The circuit is used to produce a voltage at A which is between 6 V and 0 V. The two horizontal lines are known as the 'supply rails' as they are connected directly to the battery or power supply.

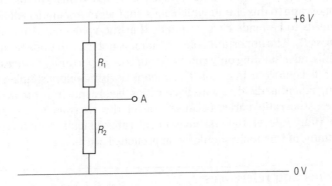

8.22 The potential divider circuit

To understand how this circuit works, it is normal to assume that the current drawn by the connection to A is negligible, as the device attached here draws very little current. Hence the current in both resistors *must be the same*. However pupils who have a 'series' concept of electric current, that is that current diminishes after it has been through every device, cannot begin to understand this circuit.

Even if they do appreciate this, they often have an alternative model of the behaviour of voltages in a circuit which is not correct. All voltages in any electric circuit are measured with reference to an arbitrary zero. The top supply rail is said to be at 6 V because the potential difference, measured in volts, between this rail and the bottom rail is 6 V. If the potential difference between the top of R_1 and A is 4 V, then the potential difference between A and the 0 V rail must be 2 V, that is the voltages add, so that in this specific case

$$V_R + V_R = 6 \text{ V}$$

The real difficulty comes when the top resistance R_1 changes because it is a light-dependent resistor or a thermistor. Now, in order to understand the circuit fully it is necessary to apply the relationship $V = IR$, have the correct model of the behaviour of current in a circuit and a satisfactory understanding of voltage. The argument can be summarised as follows.

Voltage across $R_1 = I \times R_1$
Voltage across $R_2 = I \times R_2$

Dividing one by the other gives

$$\frac{\text{Voltage across } R_1 = I \times R_1}{\text{Voltage across } R_2 = I \times R_2}$$

But the current in both resistors is the *same*, so this reduces to

$$\frac{\text{Voltage across } R_1 = R_1}{\text{Voltage across } R_2 = R_2}$$

This shows that the ratio of voltages is the ratio of the resistances. If the top resistor is a large resistor, most of the voltage will be across this. This introduces the concept of ratio to this circuit which adds another mathematical difficulty. Finally it needs to be made clear to pupils that the voltage at A equals the voltage across R_2. The important point is that it is not easy to understand this circuit. A full understanding only comes through an opportunity to investigate and discuss its behaviour in detail. This means devising many simple experiments, using potential dividers with fixed ratios, before moving onto arrangements where the ratio varies because one of the resistors is an LDR or thermistor. Many A-level students have considerable difficulty with this circuit so the teaching of this topic should be approached with care.

Notes and references

There are many books on electronics and it is often difficult for the uninitiated to know what is an appropriate book. The introduction given here is a minimal survival guide and teachers should look to other books[9] for more detailed explanation of some of these ideas if needed.

1 Bevis G. (1985) 'Should electronics be banned from school physics?' *Physics Education* **20**, **3**, 109–12.
2 Black P. & Harrison G. (1985) *In Place of Confusion.* Loughborough College of Technology.
3 The most notable kits that use this approach are (i) The *Alpha System* (ii) *Electronics 11–13* and *Electronics 13–16* and (iii) *Microelectronics for All.* These are all available from Unilab Ltd, Blackburn, Lancs.
4 The *Microelectronics for All* kit has an extensive set of publications accompanying it which includes pupil work cards and a teachers' guide which includes answers to all the problems and assessment sheets.
5 Geddes M. (1983) *Electronic Systems*, Peregrinus Ltd.
6 This chart is available from Pictorial Charts Educational Trust, 37 Kirchen Rd, London W13.
7 Foxcroft G. E., Lewis J. L. & Summers M. K. (1986) *Electronics.* Longmans.
8 The concept of voltage is the one that non-specialist physics teachers reported as causing the most difficulty in teaching in a recent study.
9 Three books in ascending order of difficulty are recommended.
Duncan T. (1985) *Electronics for Today and Tomorrow.* John Murray.
Duncan T. *Success with Electronics.* John Murray.
Hartley M. (1985) *A Practical Introduction to Electronics.* (2nd ed.) Cambridge University Press.

9 Resources for physics teaching

'If it's biology it moves, if it's chemistry it stinks and if it's physics it doesn't work . . .'

This old adage represents a succinct summary of many pupils' experience of practical work and demonstrations in physics. There is nothing more demoralising for pupils and teachers than experiments that fail to demonstrate their purported intentions. Yet practical work forms a substantial fraction of any child's experience of physics. What is the rationale and justification for this and what can teachers do to ensure that the equipment achieves its intentions?

Undoubtedly the predominant influence on the use of practical work in physics can be traced to Armstrong[1] who mounted a sustained attack on the didactic methods of the time. Armstrong had a vision of experimental work by the child as an original activity which would lead to a full understanding of the theory and gave rise to the concept of the *heuristic* method in science education, otherwise known as the 'discovery method'. Armstrong's ideas faded from popularity in the mid-1920s and it is not till the advent of the Nuffield courses in the 1960s that some of his ideas began to re-emerge. The Nuffield authors held the view that the laboratory and practical work would provide an opportunity for the pupil to be a 'physicist for a day'. Student experimentation is to be encouraged and there is a stress on personal discovery. The importance of this is illustrated by the fact that no student texts were published as the authors wanted to get away from the concept of the 'right result' which pervaded traditional physics courses of the time. However the authors have argued that they were not advocating the total use of the discovery method but instead a form of guided heurism. It is this attitude which still pervades much of the practical work in modern physics courses. As many teachers were to find, there are several problems with this approach. First, this method takes time that is not often available. Pupils must be allowed to perform experiments, and to make and learn from mistakes. However there is really little chance that students can really discover for themselves some of the great ideas of physics given the limited time and the nature of school physics apparatus. This apparatus is designed to illustrate general principles. It is not the apparatus of the research physicist looking for accuracy and reliability. This does not mean it is poor, but that its function is somewhat different. A much more fundamental objection is that presented by Novak[2] which is that discovery learning is not effective as it often leads to rote learning. The pupil learns how to perform the experiment and not the answer to the more important question which is 'Why does it behave this way?'

The effect is notable in the art of coarse car repairs. The essential method is to 'discover' which wire/plug/part to twiddle to get the car going again. Very few

115

ever go on to answer the higher order question of why it is that particular wire. Similarly, pupils were to 'learn' what you had to do to get the answer required by the teacher, yet very few were ever to understand why you did it that way. The positive side of this was that, for the first time for a long period of time, a re-evaluation of practical work occurred and schools were given substantial funds to invest in practical apparatus. The real flaw was in the concept of guided discovery. Practical activity in the classroom presents to the student a mass of stimuli and detail. The way a student observes the world, and what is seen as being relevant to a particular investigation, depends on the student's previous experience. If the student has no concept of what it is that they are expected to see then they simply fail to see it. Students looking for Brownian motion down a microscope fail to observe the particles moving because their concept of 'tiny white specks of light' fails to match that of the teachers. Similarly you cannot recognise constellations in the night sky unless you have been given a diagram-matic representation of the pattern you are looking for.

What then is the rationale for practical work in physics? Woolnough and Allsop[3] have argued that it is essential to cut the 'Gordian knot' that currently constrains practical work to the teaching of scientific theory. The pupil needs a pre-existing model of an electric current to make sense of the multitude of observations that can be made with a circuit board. This model is often best learnt through a mixture of demonstration and discussion rather than any attempt at empirical guided discovery by practical work. They see three fundamental aims which are central to the nature of scientific activity which justify the use of practical work. These they define as

- O developing practical scientific skills;
- O being a problem-solving scientist;
- O getting a 'feel for phenomena' and developing the tacit knowledge of the scientist.

This scheme fails to include experiments introduced by teachers which act as 'problems' for the children in challenging their 'alternative concepts'. However the important point about their statement is that it represents a long overdue attempt to redefine and clarify the value and point of practical work. It is much simpler to demonstrate Newton's Second Law with a VELA[4] and an interruptible light beam and obtain simple and accurate results without the welter of confusion generated by the associated endless streams of tape and noise. Ticker-tapes and trolleys can then be used for the purpose to which they are well suited which is developing a 'tacit' understanding of the graphical representation of motion.

It is also important that teachers appreciate the importance of any experi-mental work they or their pupils perform. Joan Solomon[5] rightly states that 'care and intelligent persistence should be rewarded by significant results'. The lack of importance attached to this has led to the myth that 'if it's physics, it doesn't work'. Solomon rightly argues that disappointing demonstrations are seen as duds and no amount of discussion of error is likely to compensate this. If the experiment fails to provide reasonable results, then it is sensible to look for alternative methods of presentation. More importantly though, it is important to realise that the successful use of much physics apparatus depends on a good working knowledge of devices and the 'tools of the trade'. This only comes through practice and it must be emphasised that it is essential to test physics experiments before using them with the class.

The 'tools of the trade'

The apparatus used by the physics teacher for practical work should be appropriate and relevant. It is still sad to find schools using ammeters and voltmeters that look positively pre-war in their design for developing the skill of reading an analogue meter when nearly all modern instruments are digital in design. Physics apparatus should reflect the technology of the times if the subject is to avoid becoming historical. What follows is an outline of common pieces of physics apparatus and some of the problems in their operation that it is essential to look for.

Power supplies

Low voltage supplies

A good working knowledge of these devices is essential for any serious practical work since they are used in such a wide variety of experiments. The power supply needs to be able to supply a range of voltages from 0 to 12 V, preferably in 1 V steps but 2 V steps are acceptable. They should be fitted with a 'trip switch' which trips if the supply is accidentally shorted, and they should be capable of delivering a.c. or d.c. The a.c. supply has yellow terminals while the d.c. supply has a red and a black terminal. Finally it is useful if they have a locking nut on the voltage selector so that the voltage can be locked to a preset limit preventing the pupils from increasing the voltage and damaging the equipment. It is important to be aware of the fact that the d.c. voltage produced by these power supplies is said to be 'unsmoothed'. The a.c. voltage has merely been rectified so that the voltage still varies from zero to the maximum positive voltage a hundred times a second (figure 9.1). This means that these power supplies are not acceptable substitutes for a 'smoothed' (that is steady) power

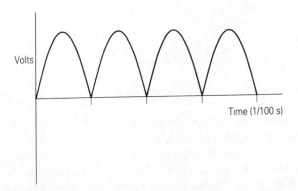

9.1 Rectified unsmoothed alternating voltage from a typical power supply

supply, as the voltage is not constant. A smoothed supply is needed for all work with electronic circuits and this is most simply provided by using batteries. Unsmoothed power supplies will not operate amplifiers. The supply can be 'smoothed' by adding what is called a 'smoothing unit' which is often sold separately.

Most power supplies sold these days are fairly rugged and dependable. Problems arise for the teacher when pupils inadvertently or deliberately trip the cut-out. It is easy to miss this and teachers are advised to look first at this if the supply appears not to be functioning. Another common mistake is to make use of the a.c. supply when d.c. is needed. This rarely does any harm but normally means that the circuit does not work. The modern low voltage power supply is a fairly indestructible item and requires a particularly malevolent pupil to cause it harm.

Experiments in electromagnetism require a very low voltage supply of 2 V maximum which is effectively capable of being shorted by connecting a wire across the terminals. This will normally cause the 'trip switch' of the standard low voltage supply to cut out. These power supplies are normally supplied separately and are essential for serious work in electromagnetism. The maximum current they can deliver is limited to about 8 A and hence they do not have a 'trip switch'. For a really spectacular demonstration of the magnetic effect of an electromagnetic current, teachers are advised to use a car battery and a thick piece of copper cable, such as a car starter motor cable (figure 9.2).

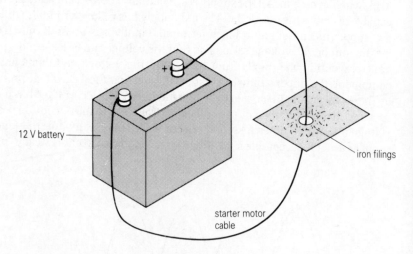

9.2 The electromagnetic field of a large current

Wearing rubber gloves to protect against sparks, the loose end should be thrust onto the terminal. The high current (≈ 200 A) has the effect of rapidly orientating the iron filings to the magnetic field and provides an effective demonstration. Provided the cable is not coiled up, there is no danger of shock as the voltage is only 12 V. The sparks are caused by the heating effect of the high current.

118

High voltage supplies

A few experiments in physics require the use of a high voltage power supply (EHT or Extra High Tension) capable of providing a voltage up to a maximum of 5000 V. Such experiments are notably the 'shuttling ball' experiment and the spark counter for detecting ionising radiations. Despite the apparently high voltage they are not particularly dangerous. It is important to remember that it is the size of the current that causes heart seizure and it is normally thought that it requires a current of 0.1 A to do this, though sensitivity to electric shock varies from individual to individual. High voltage supplies have a high internal resistance which limits the current they are capable of delivering to a maximum of 1 mA. However this would still be sufficient to cause a significant shock and further protection is generally given by providing two outputs as shown in figure 9.3. The 'direct' output is capable

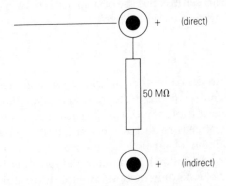

9.3 Direct and indirect outputs of an EHT supply

of delivering a higher current than the indirect output which has an extra 50 MΩ of resistance internally to ensure that the maximum current delivered is 0.1 mA. Teachers are advised to use the indirect output for all experiments as a safety precaution as there is no necessity to use the other output. Even less dangerous than the high voltage supply above is the Van de Graaff generator which is only capable of delivering a maximum current of 1 μA. The Van de Graaff generator produces very high voltages indeed, in the region of 100 000 V, but as soon as any current is drawn from the supply, the voltage drops rapidly to zero. The high voltage is capable of causing air molecules to ionise, leading to sparks and other spectacular effects. Touching the charged sphere causes a shock because the voltage drives a very small current through the user to earth but it is considered harmless for a normally healthy individual. *It is not advisable to let children with weak hearts handle this machine.*

The most dangerous power supply is the 0 to 300 V power supply used with the 'fine beam' tube to demonstrate deflection of an electron beam. This power supply is capable of delivering 50 mA at 300 V which can be lethal. This power supply is essential for this experiment but should be treated with due respect, and care should be taken to avoid touching any exposed metal terminals. Because of the potential danger, pupils must not be allowed to use this apparatus.

However it must be pointed out that the most dangerous power supply available to the physics teacher is the mains power supply which is at 240 V and capable of delivering very large currents indeed. It is the responsibility of the physics teacher to ensure that all the mains apparatus is correctly wired and that faulty plugs and sockets are repaired promptly. Ideally physics laboratories should have a 'residual current device', RCD, (also called an 'earth leakage circuit breaker', ELCB) and a master switch which controls all the sockets in the laboratory. The former automatically trips as soon as a minimal current is detected in the earth; the latter provides the teacher with a manual means of rapidly isolating the mains in the case of an electrocution. Mains electricity should always be treated with respect. A useful strategy when handling suspect mains equipment is to keep one hand in a pocket. This ensures that, in the event of electrocution, the current will not flow across the heart to earth and reduces the risk of heart seizure. But the best advice is to turn off the power before touching anything that could be 'live'.

Ticker timers

These devices were introduced by the Nuffield physics courses as a cheap recording device which enabled pupils to record distance and time on a strip of paper tape. The advantage of the tape is that it can easily be cut into 'ten-tick' strips which can then be arranged in a normal block graph. This provides a useful visual record of the motion of an object which acts as a suitable introduction to the graphical representation of motion and its analysis. The only alternative to this method of recording motion is to use the technique of 'multi-flash' photography.

The main problem with ticker timers is that they suffer from simple mechanical problems of which the teacher needs to be aware.

Double dotting

This is generally caused by resonance of the vibrating arm so that the arm actually hits the carbon paper twice as it vibrates. Cures for this are to reduce the voltage of the power supply, or to adjust the arm using a screwdriver. Sometimes these are not successful and pupils need to be told to consider the pairs of dots as one dot.

No dots appearing

This is a very common problem and is generally due to the fact that the ticker timer is one that uses a drawing pin to position the carbon slip. The drawing pin has been pushed right into the cork and prevents rotation of the carbon slip which rapidly becomes worn out. Lifting the drawing pin slightly allows the carbon to rotate and dots should appear again. A close inspection of the carbon paper is required if this is the problem. Another difficulty is that occasionally pupils use a voltage on the power supply which is too low; simply using a higher voltage cures the problem.

It is important to mention that this device has been overused in many physics courses to the extent that for some pupils the main memory of physics has become one of a classroom full of noisy vibrating ticker timers. The latest models of this device are substantially quieter and use pressure sensitive paper which eliminates the need for a carbon paper. However, it is simply one device in a repertoire of instruments that physics teachers have for recording time and motion. The necessity for it is best introduced through attempting to time how long it takes a block of wood to fall from the laboratory window. This enjoyable experiment illustrates that, even with modern digital watches that can measure times to ± 0.01 second, the pupils will not be able to agree about a common time and some more effective measuring technique is needed. At this point the ticker timer can be introduced.

However there is a very strong argument that there is little point in using the ticker timer to verify Newton's Second Law. The experiment is inherently full of so many potential errors that it is more a matter of luck than experimental skill that determines whether an individual obtains results that confirm Newton's law. Friction compensation is generally only very approximate and should be done with the tape running, which is an additional source of friction. Very few individuals can maintain a constant force with the elastics and it is difficult to see how this can be justified as a useful experimental skill. These days the advent of the VELA[4] and other devices which can provide direct measurements of acceleration means that Newton's laws are more effectively demonstrated by the teacher, or that this experiment is part of a circus of experiments on motion which the pupils do themselves. The skill of using a modern device like this is something which is likely to have more utility in later life than the ability to stretch an elastic band to a constant length while running alongside an accelerating trolley!

Other techniques of recording the motion of a moving object include multi-flash photography and using a scaler-timer which is able to measure time to an accuracy of $\frac{1}{1000}$ of a second, allowing very accurate determinations of g, the gravitational acceleration.

Multi-flash photography

The essential principle of this technique is that of repeatedly photographing the position of an object at constant time intervals. There are two ways of doing this. Either the object can be repeatedly viewed by placing a slit in front of the camera at regular intervals or the object can be repeatedly illuminated with a stroboscope, again at constant time intervals (figure 9.4). Of the two methods the former is simpler as it can be done with the lights on whereas the latter method requires a dark room. In both cases the image is recorded onto the same negative or print. Since none of the other objects move, the images contain a succession of images of the moving object all separated at regular time intervals. Providing a suitable scale has also been photographed so that distances on the photograph can be converted to real distances, the velocity and acceleration of the object can be calculated.

However, the problem with the technique is that it necessitates the rapid development of the film in the class, or a delay until the successive lesson while the film is developed in between. Developing the film in class requires a black bag, a developing tank and some developer and fixer. In addition the teacher needs the skill required to open a cassette in the dark and load it into a tank. This

121

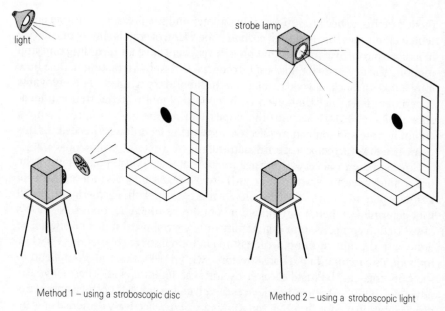

Method 1 – using a stroboscopic disc   Method 2 – using a stroboscopic light

Photographing a falling object

9.4 Apparatus for multi-flash photography

is not really difficult but it does require several practice attempts before willingly attempting to do it publicly in front of a large group of expectant pupils. The alternative method of introducing the 'ones I took yesterday just in case this didn't work' is not very convincing either. The simplest method for the inexperienced teacher is to use a Polaroid camera with a black and white film. Polaroid film is rated at 3000 ASA[6] which means that it is affected by very dim light and is ideally suited to this kind of work. Unfortunately modern polaroid cameras do not have the facility to hold the shutter open for as long as the shutter is depressed though it is not difficult to find older cameras in second-hand shops and jumble sales. Covering the 'magic eye' of these cameras causes the shutter to stay open as long as it is depressed. The great advantage is that the results can be produced almost instantaneously and that it is possible to record the motion of a falling object ten times on one print. The object is dropped first on the far left as viewed in the viewfinder. The experiment is then repeated moving the object to the right a small distance so that the final fall takes place in a position on the far right of the viewfinder. The print can then be cut up so that each pupil has his own record of the event. In addition, this technique generally provides remarkably accurate results for such things as g, the gravitational acceleration.

The object needs to be highly reflecting, which can be done by using a polished metal ball or by covering the object in aluminium. Alternatively, a luminous object may be used[7]. One of the most effective falling objects is a 1.5 V battery with lamp holder and bulb attached. It survives most falls provided that a box with cloth padding is placed beneath and is an excellent luminous source for photographing. (No other source of illumination is needed.) Like most physics experiments, success depends upon the willingness to practise a few times in advance, but the effort is more than worthwhile as evidenced by the excitement on the faces of the pupils when the print appears. The other advantage is that it has the air of being something which is the result of their own efforts.

The oscilloscope

There is not space here to provide a thorough introduction to the use of this device and an explanation of all the controls. Modern oscilloscopes seem to the unfamiliar to be a sophisticated array of knobs and switches which are designed to obscure and confuse rather than assist. The essential thing for the novice to understand is, that like much modern technological equipment, *the only way of breaking it is to drop it.* Otherwise it is impossible to do much harm.

What is an oscilloscope? A conceptual understanding of the nature of this instrument is much more useful than any detailed knowledge of all the facilities on one machine. The oscilloscope consists of a cathode ray tube with an electron beam which is focussed to produce a single spot on the screen. This spot vertically can be deflected vertically by applying a voltage to the inputs of the scope. The size of the deflection is dependent on the setting of the knob which is labelled 'volts/cm' or 'y gain'. Hence the oscilloscope can be used to measure voltages by measuring the deflection of the spot and using the setting on the volts/cm control to calculate the voltage. It is possible to shift the position of the spot vertically with a control labelled 'y shift'. Many modern oscilloscopes provide two spots so that two measurements can be made independently and simultaneously. A schematic representation of such an oscilloscope is shown in figure 9.5. It is this conceptual representation that is needed for the successful use of the oscilloscope. The user needs to approach each oscilloscope with the intention of making the connection between this mental model and the actual implementation which varies.

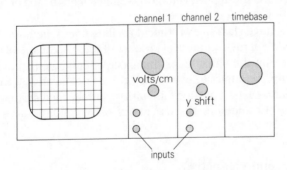

9.5 Schematic representation of a modern oscilloscope

In addition the spot can be driven horizontally at constant speed by the electronics in the machine. The speed is controlled by a knob labelled 'timebase'. On modern oscilloscopes it can go as fast as 1 cm/1 μs. When the spot is driven sideways it no longer appears as a spot on the screen because of a persistence of the image on the screen and persistence of vision in the eye and it appears as a continuous line. The oscilloscope then becomes ideal for demon-

123

strating transient electrical events which happen very rapidly. For example, it is ideally suited to displaying the electrical signal produced by a microphone and the voltage generated by the mains.

The main problem experienced with oscilloscopes is finding the beam which has somehow disappeared. This generally involves a systematic approach of checking (i) the brightness to ensure the spot is not too dim to be seen, (ii) the y shift to ensure that the spot has not been moved off the bottom or top of the screen and (iii) the x shift to ensure that it has not been shifted off the side of the screen. Adjusting these controls should normally bring the beam into view. If all else fails though, it is possible that the triggering mode needs adjustment. A good tip is to mark the settings of the controls with a chinagraph pencil when the spot is centred on the screen for future use.

The trigger facility prevents the spot from sweeping across the screen until a voltage is registered at the inputs. The effect of this is that the sweep of the beam and the voltage being measured are synchronised so that the trace always occupies the same position on the screen. This makes it mush easier to view and take measurements from. There is normally a knob labelled 'trigger' which should be adjusted to cause the beam to trigger correctly. The situation is more complicated with double beam oscilloscopes as the beam can be triggered by Channel 1, Channel 2 or an external pulse. It is pointless to attempt to trigger the scope off Channel 2 when the voltage of interest is being fed to Channel 1 and teachers should look carefully to see which input they have selected for triggering if they are having difficulty obtaining a steady trace or any trace at all.

The final difficulty that can cause problems is the selector switch next to the inputs which offers the choice of d.c., a.c. or ground. This should be set to the nature of the voltage being used. Attempts to measure d.c. voltages with this switch set to a.c. will not work though the reverse of this will. Grounding the beam earths the inputs so that no voltage is applied and is useful for recovering the beam on the screen if the applied voltage has shifted it off the top or bottom of the screen.

Some schools will have class sets of student oscilloscopes which are essentially simplified models of the commercial product. If these are available, then they should be used by the students as this piece of equipment provides a valuable opportunity for pupils to experience the use of relatively modern equipment which has at least a passing familiarity from the media exposure of hospital technology. In addition, the use of the oscilloscope is a valuable experimental skill.

Ammeters and voltmeters

Most physics classrooms require a voltmeter capable of measuring to 15 V and an ammeter that is capable of measuring to 1 A. However, because of the need to measure small currents of 1 mA as well as large ones, it is common to find a range of meters which measure to different ranges in physics classrooms or one meter with a range of shunts which plug in and alter the range of reading. Most meters in schools are still analogue meters with a scale that is subdivided by further divisions. The Assessment of Performance Unit[8] have shown how difficult pupils find it to read these devices, particularly when the divisions of the scale are based on fifths of a unit rather than tenths of a unit. For the physics teacher it is simply a question of ensuring that the right meter is selected for the practical work and it is better to err on the side of caution and pick a range that is initially too high so that the meter will not be damaged by excessive current or voltage. Also, most meters are designed for the measurement of d.c. voltages and currents and will not measure a.c. Meters for measuring a.c. usually have terminals that are yellow rather than red and black.

Many new meters used in society and industry are digital meters. They are obviously substantially easier to read as no interpretation of an analogue scale is required. In addition they have substantially improved accuracy as they require a minimal current to determine the reading and are generally capable of reading a wide range of currents and voltages from 0.001 to 10 amps or volts. They are another example of what Pacey[9] has called the 'deskilling of society by technology'. Such meters are now widely available for schools and it is hoped that schools will not hesitate to purchase them where funds are available. Lack of competence at the redundant skill of being able to read an analogue meter will no longer prohibit pupils from direct experience of the idea that the current in a circuit is exactly the same all the way round which is one of the fundamental aims of a basic electricity course. It is difficult to find any logical justification for the continued use of analogue-measuring equipment when suitable alternatives are available. Digital meters also have the advantage of being suitable for demonstration purposes since it is possible to read the digits up to 5 m away. Their one major disadvantage is that they lack any sense of the dynamic. It is more difficult to gain a rapid visual impression of the rate of change from watching a set of numbers change compared to watching a needle drop.

Unilab market a demonstration digital meter which can be loaded into the carriage of a slide projector for large-scale demonstrations, and increased use of digital meters will force schools into using such meters if they are to maintain any consistency of approach. The important point for teachers is that demonstrations of the behaviour of electric circuits require large meters that can be read from reasonable distances. The standard student meter is not suitable and an alternative should be sought.

The scaler ratemeter

This instrument comes in many different shapes and sizes from the early 1950s valve operated versions to the latter day all-singing-and-dancing machines that led one caustic observer to mutter that they look as though they need a degree to operate them. Fortunately this is not true as the machine can be simplified to its basic systems. These are a counter (scaler), an internal clock producing 1000 pulses each second, and a set of electronic gates that stop and start the counter going. A simplified system diagram is shown in figure 9.6.

A major use of such instruments is in radioactivity where the pulses from the Geiger–Müller tube are fed to the counter which counts the number of pulses detected. The scaler ratemeter contains a high voltage d.c. power supply to

125

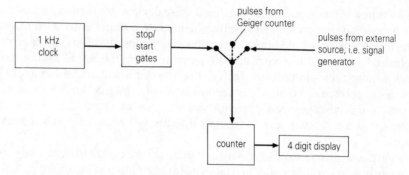

9.6 System diagram of a scaler ratemeter

which the tube is attached and the voltage adjusted for normal working. For most commercial Geiger–Müller tubes this is 400 V. The modern instruments provide the facility to count for periods of 1 s, 10 s or 100 s before they reset the display and start counting again. This is useful in radioactivity experiments where the count is being monitored over a period of time. Alternatively there is a switch which permits a single reading to be taken for one of the above periods. Older instruments usually only take uninterrupted single readings. The advantage of the older instruments is that they use an older type of display based on valves containing neon and an electromechanical counter. This has the advantage of giving a very clear audio-visual representation of the quantity of radiation being detected as a strong source causes the lights to rotate and counter to audibly click. Liquid crystal displays lack this and the manufacturers provide a speaker which will blip as a pulse is detected. This should be switched on, or connected if it is an external speaker, as it provides a clear audible sensation of the rate of decay. Many of the modern instruments provide a connector to which a solid state detector can be attached. Solid state detectors are supposedly good at detecting alpha radiation but they are notoriously unreliable and teachers are advised not to use them.

The second use of this device is for counting the pulses from a 1 kHz clock and timing events which are started and stopped electronically. There is a button on the front which allows the selection between 'timing' and 'counting'. This should be set to 'timing'. The timer is normally started by shorting together the 'start' terminals. This can be done electronically by using a circuit containing a photodiode which conducts when light falls on it. Similarly the timer is stopped by shorting the stop terminals together. One of the standard experiments using this apparatus is to measure the time for an object to fall over 1 m. This uses some simple apparatus which is called '*g* by free fall' and makes use of the stop/ start terminals to time the event (figure 9.7). When the metal ball is released the stop terminals are no longer connected while the start terminals are. This sets the timer going and it continues till the ball hits the metal trapdoor at the bottom which breaks the electrical contact between the start terminals which stops the timer. The peculiar reverse logic of this arrangement works very well and very accurate values for *g* can be obtained which impress the most dubious pupil.

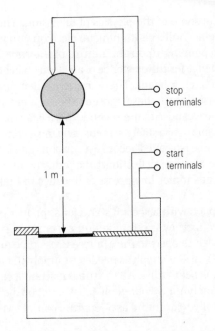

9.7 Circuit arrangement for measuring *g* by free fall

There are many other uses for such a timer. One of the simplest is to use it with two push switches to measure reaction times. A more sophisticated use is possible with the model marketed by Unilab. This has a pair of switches which allow the user to select a range of pulses which can initiate the starting and stopping of the timer. One selection allows this to be done with a microphone. A sharp pulse produced by hitting an aluminium block with a hammer, sets the timer going and it is stopped when the pulse reaches the second microphone at a typical distance of 3 m. This gives a direct reading for the time of travel of the sound pulse from which the speed of sound can be calculated directly. Again this experiment normally yields an accurate value for the speed of sound.

Finally the modern versions of this instrument have a third facility which allows the instrument to measure the frequency of an electrical oscillation. This has many potential uses in discussing resonance and musical notes. A microphone can be connected directly to the inputs and the frequency of 'middle C' measured. A note one octave higher can then be played to demonstrate that it is twice the frequency. Notes of the same frequency but different amplitudes can be played to demonstrate that the pitch of a note is determined solely by the frequency and not the amplitude.

Teltron tubes

As with much physics apparatus, the term 'Teltron tube' is the manufacturer's name used to describe a generic set of apparatus used for illustrating the behaviour of electron beams. Since the modern television tube makes use of an electron beam to 'draw' its picture on the screen, these 'tubes' provide a useful demonstration of some of the physics of television. They are really specially made evacuated glass bulbs containing an electron gun assembly and a target which varies depending upon the nature of the tube. Their primary aim is to show some evidence for the existence of an electron beam and to demonstrate the properties of such a beam. There are two safety implications; first, high voltages are used, and these require special care as the terminals on most Telton tubes are exposed; and second, there is a risk of the tube imploding, so that it is advisable to use safety screens. The most commonly used tubes are the Maltese Cross tube (so called because it contains an electrode shaped like a Maltese cross), the electron deflection tube, and the fine beam tube, which contains hydrogen gas under low pressure in order to make the path of the beam visible.

These tubes are normally supplied with a special stand for supporting them and need to be treated with care as they are fragile and expensive. An EHT power supply (0–5000 V) is needed to operate the Maltese Cross tube and the electron deflection tube, while a 0–300 V supply is needed to supply the higher current required to operate the fine beam tube. All the tubes contain a cathode at the rear which is heated by applying a voltage of 6.3 V (a.c. or d.c.) to it (figure 9.8). This voltage is normally to be found as a separate pair of terminals

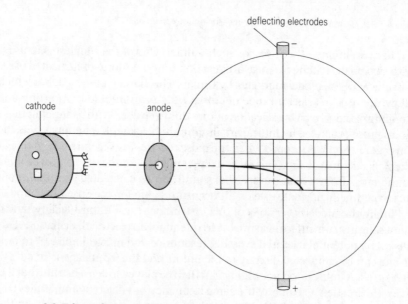

9.8 Teltron electron deflection tube

on the high voltage supply. This should be connected first and switching on the power supply should result in a visible glow being produced by the heated cathode in the neck of the tube. Turning the power supply off, the high voltage can now be connected. It is normal to set the variable high voltage supply to zero volts and attach the positive terminal to the terminal protruding from the neck of the tube. The negative terminal is attached to either one of the terminals provided at the rear for the cathode. A third connection is often made now

128

between the negative terminal on the supply and the green earth terminal. This ensures that the cathode is effectively held at zero volts. In addition, in the case of the Maltese Cross tube and the electron deflection tube, a connection should be made between the anode and the electrodes in the middle of the glass tube so that they are at the same voltage as the anode. This ensures that the electrons are still accelerated after passing through the aperture in the anode.

The voltage of the supply can now be raised. In the case of the Maltese Cross tube, a green outline of the cross should appear on the fluorescent screen at the front of the tube. There will already be a yellow outline due to the light emitted by the heaters. What the tube demonstrates is that something is being attracted to the positive anode which effectively travels in straight lines and causes the screen to fluoresce on striking it. In addition bringing a small magnet adjacent to the tube causes the outline to deflect. What does this evidence tell us about the nature of such rays? It shows that the particles emitted by the cathode are negatively charged and easily deflected and in doing so illustrates the principle of magnetic deflection of electron beams. A television picture is produced by magnetically deflecting an electron beam from the top left-hand corner across the screen to form 625 lines, successively descending one line at a time. This is done 25 times a second so that the images merge due to persistence of vision.

The electron deflection tube contains a rectangular grid sandwiched between two electrodes placed at a shallow angle to the beam. The beam from the anode strikes the grid causing it to fluoresce so that the path can be seen. If both the electrodes are at the same potential (voltage), having been connected to the positive anode, the beam continues in a straight line. If one plate is attached to the anode and the other to the negative, the beam deflects in a parabolic path towards the positive electrode. Reversing the connections to the electrodes, reverses the deflection. Apart from demonstrating that the beam consists of negatively charged particles, this tube also demonstrates the electrostatic deflection of the beam which is used in the cathode ray oscilloscope to deflect the beam. It is also possible to calculate the ratio of charge to mass for the particles by measuring the beam, but this is not something that should be attempted with pupils of average ability.

The fine beam tube is different from the previous two in that it is not totally evacuated since it contains hydrogen gas under low pressure which is ionised as the electron beam passes through it. The resultant recombination of the ions to form atoms leads to the emission of light which makes the path of the beam visible. The tube normally has two sets of cathodes, one at the rear of the neck of the tube for directing the beam across the tube and one at the front of the neck for producing a beam in the vertical direction for deflection by magnetic fields. A small switch at the rear allows selection between the cathodes. This tube is normally used for demonstrating the magnetic deflection of the electron beam into a circular path by a magnetic field produced by a pair of adjacent coils. It makes a clear and effective demonstration when done in the dark but takes some care and effort to ensure its successful operation.[10]

Notes and references

1 For a full account of the work of Armstrong see Van Pragh G. (ed.) (1973) *H. E. Armstrong and Science Education*. John Murray, London.
2 Novak J. D. (1978) 'An alternative to Piagetian psychology for science and mathematics education'. *Studies in Science Education*, **5**, 1–30.
3 Woolnough B. & Allsop T. (1985) *Practical Work in Science*. Cambridge University Press.
4 The VELA is the Versatile Laboratory Aid sold by Educational Electronics. Bedford. With a physics EPROM fitted, which is available from Instrumentation Software Ltd, 7 Gledhow Wood Avenue, Leeds LS8 1NY, direct measurements of acceleration of an object can be obtained.
5 Solomon J. (1980) *Teaching Children in the Laboratory*. Croom Helm, London.
6 The ASA rating of a film provides a measure of how fast the chemical will react to light. The higher the number, the faster it reacts and the less light is needed to correctly expose it. Normal black-and-white film is 125 ASA so the Polaroid film will take photographs in extremely poorly lit conditions.
7 Foster S. (1980) *Polaroid strobe photos at 2p a go?*, School Science Review **217**, June 1980, p. 736.
8 *Electricity at Age 15*. (1984) Assessment of Performance Unit. DES, HMSO.
9 Pacey Arnold (1983) *The Culture of Technology*, Open University Press.
10 See *Revised Nuffield Physics, Teacher's Guide, Year V*, pages 27–9, for further details.

10 New technology in the physics laboratory

What does the new technology have to offer the non-specialist teacher? Besieged by a sea of uncertainty about the content of the lesson, it would at first seem senseless to attempt to use some new-fangled piece of high technology that will only increase the confusion of teacher and taught. However there are several reasons for pausing to think of some of the possible advantages that may help to inspire confidence in the pupils and make the learning more valuable and meaningful. These reasons can be summarised as follows.

Improved dependability and accuracy

There is nothing more disappointing to many pupils than physics experiments that fail to work effectively. Just as 'real' scientists seek to test their hypotheses about the world by experiment, the physics teacher seeks through demonstrations to illustrate physical concepts and provide evidence for their validity. Experiments that fail force teachers into the position of producing excuses such as 'It was working before the lesson', or 'This apparatus isn't very good' or 'If it had worked, this is the result we would have got anyway'. A slightly more defensible position is to keep a set of results from an occasion when the experiment did work effectively and produce these if the experiment fails. For the critical young pupil, such ploys are ineffective and naturally lead them to question the value of the activity. Enthusiasm is a fickle and delicate thing that must be constantly nurtured otherwise it withers. Dud experiments taught by muted apologists do not help. Modern technology provides physics teachers with powerful tools that allow them to present effective demonstrations and obtain impressive results from experiments with relative ease.

Extending the realm of the observable

Many physical phenomena discussed and illustrated in physics teaching are relatively transient and difficult to capture because of the short time scale involved. The wave pattern produced by a microphone, the voltage induced in a coil by a magnet and the change in current through a light bulb as a voltage is applied are examples. Modern devices have the ability to take several thousand readings a second which allows such phenomena to be investigated fully.

Increased simplicity

The ability of many interfaces to make rapid, simple and accurate measurements of such quantities as time, velocity, acceleration and temperature allows one instrument to be used to provide direct measurements of the speed of sound, the acceleration due to gravity, the relationship between force and acceleration and many other examples.

More 'professional' results

Many of the interfacing packages have the facility incorporated that transfers the graphical output to a printer. This produces a permanent high quality record of the experiment which is particularly useful for pupils with poor graphical skills. But, in addition, it provides for pupils the sensation of working with equipment that is technologically sophisticated and has the ability to manipulate data and present it in a quality comparable to that observed in newspapers and magazines.

However new technology in any shape or form often generates initial fear and uncertainty. This need not be so. The more advanced the technology, the more robust and simple it is to use and the less there is to fear. Change always generates fear because it threatens our image of ourselves. Claxton[1] highlights this in defining what he calls the 4 'C's. People often operate on the belief that they should be *competent, consistent,* in *control* and *comfortable*. The problem is that these 'four commandments' are the exact antitheses of what teachers commonly require of learners, and of what they feel themselves when dealing with new ways of teaching! Children should not be denied an educationally valuable experience because teachers fear their own ability to demonstrate something of value and are reluctant to change with the times. The essential decisions that have to be made by teachers about any new experimental method are

(*a*) does it genuinely extend the experience of the pupils?
(*b*) does it offer greater and appropriate accuracy and sensitivity?
(*c*) does it provide a novel opportunity to exercise information skills in presenting, analysing and interpreting data?
(*e*) is it fun?

If the answer to one of these questions is yes, then the teacher should seriously consider the use of such technology as a means of improving the quality of their teaching and the pupils' understanding.

There is insufficient space to deal here with the complete range of devices that are available. Instead, it is simpler to illustrate the previous points by discussing the potential use of one particular device, the VELA (Versatile Laboratory Aid) (figure 10.1). This microprocessor-based instrument is chosen because it represents, at present, both a commonly available device, and one with the greatest potential. There are several accessories for use in the physics laboratory and it is *not recommended* that teachers attempt to use it without these. These are the *physics EPROM,* the *light gate sensor* and the *temperature sensors*[2] and the *Data Scientific worksheets*[3]. In common with many other devices, the original manual was not sensibly written to assist the novice and is

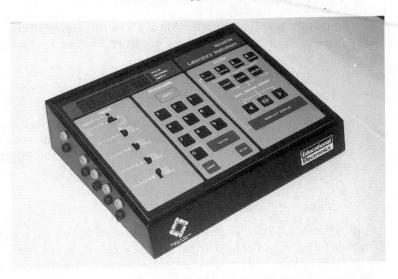

10.1 The VELA

rather off-putting. Teachers should use the worksheets and then progress to the manual.

The VELA only measures voltages. In order to measure temperature, light intensity and motion, appropriate transducers[4] are needed. Transducers are devices which convert the former quantities to a voltage which the VELA can record by converting the voltage to a binary number electronically using a micro-chip called an Analogue to Digital Converter ('A to D chip'). The VELA then stores this binary number before taking another reading. This is represented in figure 10.2 When all the readings have been taken, they can then be displayed as decimal numbers: individually on the limited alphanu-

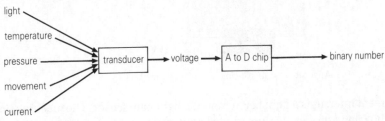

10.2 System outline of a typical interface

meric display of the machine, displayed as a graph on an oscilloscope screen, or transferred to a microcomputer[5] for graphical display and further analysis by relevant software[6]. The argument often used against such devices is that they are black boxes which, because of their complexity, obscure from the user the mechanisms by which the measurements are performed and so make the physics less accessible. The logical extension of such an argument though is that we should not use any measuring instrument in the laboratory which we cannot explain the principles of operation to children. This would automati-

133

cally preclude the use of the ammeter in junior science, particularly the modern digital version. The problem is often more the teacher's than the childrens' and the benefits should be considered carefully.

Experiments with an interface

The following is a brief description of a representative range of possible experiments with one device, chosen because they illustrate some of the arguments outlined previously. For a fuller description of the experiments, users will need to refer to the notes in the references.

Measuring acceleration

The VELA has a program that directly measures acceleration (program 69). This can be used to measure the acceleration of an object in free fall which it does by making use of a card and a light gate. The card needs a segment cut into it as illustrated in figure 10.3. As the card falls, the bottom

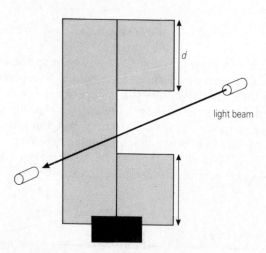

10.3 Apparatus for measuring g directly with VELA

segment interrupts a light beam from the light gate sensor. The machine times for how long the beam is interrupted with an accuracy of ± 100 μs. When the second segment passes into the beam it times how long this takes to pass through the light beam. These times can be measured directly and used to calculate the average speed of the first segment through the beam and the average speed of the second segment through the beam. From these values the change in speed can be calculated, and using the value of the time between the two interruptions of the beam the acceleration can be calculated from

$$\text{acceleration} = \frac{\text{change in velocity}}{\text{time taken}}$$

134

This is done using program 67. Program 68 repeats this but shows that the machine will calculate the two velocities, and program 69 calculates the acceleration directly. Having taken the children through the method using first program 67 followed by program 68, program 69 can then be used. In this the user inputs the value for *d* (figure 10.3) and the machine performs the calculations to determine *g*, the gravitational acceleration, and displays the result instantaneously. The acceleration of several objects of different mass due to gravity can be measured. Typically values that range from 9.6 m/s² to 10.1 m/s² are obtained. The experimental variation is due to the width of the light beam which introduces a random fluctuation in the timing. The main advantage is that a relatively accurate series of results can be obtained quickly. Use of the VELA allows the measurements to be taken simply and quickly and extends the realm of the possible in the physics laboratory. The instructions are shown in the figure 10.4.

In addition, this program can be used to demonstrate the relationship between force and acceleration easily. If the card is attached to a trolley on a friction compensated runway and the trolley is accelerated by a constant force, the acceleration of the trolley can be measured directly and typical results are shown in chapter 1 (figure 1.4).

Using the program

Type the following on the keyboard	Notes
67	This selects the program
1	This defines the way in which the timer is started. (See the notes if you are using non-stndard light gates)
ENTER	This enters the program into the machine
START	

When timing is complete

The machine displays time t_1 the time for the first segment to go through. To see t_2, press

FWD	Display shows t_2 (time for the second segment to go through)
FWD	Pressing again shows t_3 (time between readings)

10.4 Instruction summary for program 67

New technology in the physics laboratory

Measuring the velocity of sound

The traditional methods of doing this rely on the use of an oscilloscope. This necessitates that the pupils comprehend that the oscilloscope is essentially a timing device. However the VELA provides a facility to the physics teacher for measuring the time of flight of a pulse of sound directly, since it can measure the time of passage of the pulse to within $100\ \mu s$. The apparatus is set up as shown in figure 10.5[7]. This experiment uses program 65. The key presses required to enter this are shown in figure 10.6.

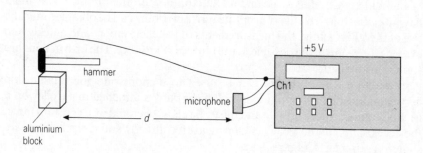

set the external/internal switch to internal and Ch1 to +250 mV

10.5 Apparatus for measuring the speed of sound

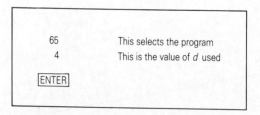

10.6 Instruction summary for program 65

A sharp, clean pulse of sound is provided by using a hammer on an aluminium block; the longer the distance from the block to the microphone the less the percentage error in the result will be. The electrical pulse produced by the contact of the hammer on the block triggers the timer and the pulse from the microphone stops it. The advantage of using such a method is that once it is set up, the result is obtained quickly. This means that several results can be taken and an average value obtained. The concept of averaging many results as a means of minimising error can be discussed. Even with only a few experiments, the error is small, and results with an accuracy of $\pm 1\%$ are obtainable. The more ambitious can attempt to measure the speed of sound in a metal rod by placing a metal rod between the source and the microphone.

Recording waveforms

This makes a useful extension experiment to perform with pupils who have used an oscilloscope to look at the waveforms produced by the sound of their own voice. The VELA has a fast transient recorder program, program 01. The microphone is connected to the channel 1 input and program 01 selected. The parameter '0' is entered which reduces the time between measurements to a minimum so that the instrument works at the fastest possible rate. The triggering should be set to 'internal' and the voltage range to ±250 mV. Talking into the microphone causes the device to record almost instantaneously.

The result is most easily displayed on an oscilloscope which needs to be connected to the analogue output with the sweep speed set to 1 ms cm. Pressing 'CH1' followed by 'scope' will lead to the waveform being displayed on the screen. Some adjustment of the trigger of the oscilloscope may be necessary to obtain a static display. This method is most useful when used to look at the note produced by a whistle and a range of musical instruments. Investigations can be done on the effect on the waveform of:

(a) two notes of the same pitch but different loudness;
(b) two notes of different pitch but the same loudness;
(c) two notes of the same pitch produced by different instruments.

Sample results are shown in figure 10.7.

This experiment provides a good example of the potential to produce a 'professional' printed record of the output. To do this, a computer, the requisite software and transfer cable are necessary. The software is loaded and run and a request to transfer data from the VELA selected. 'CH1' and 'micro' are now pressed and the data will automatically be transferred to the computer which will plot the trace on the screen. Most software programs now provide the facility to produce a printer dump of the screen display. Children can then be provided with a 'print' of their own voice which they can stick in their books or display on the wall and this is generally much appreciated.

Three experiments have been shown to illustrate the potential of this device for the physics teacher. Many more are possible with this and other computer interfaces[8] and the ASE has produced a useful booklet[9] to provide assistance for those who wish to explore that range of possible experiments with the BBC microcomputer. The Data Scientific worksheets provide 62 physics experiments that are possible with the VELA which are grouped into four areas. These are

(a) introductory worksheets (up to 14 years);
(b) secondary worksheets (13–16 years);
(c) intermediate worksheets (15–17 years);
(d) advanced worksheets (16–18 years).

The addition of a range of sensors extends the possibilities even further, and it is difficult to see how an approach to the teaching of physics that does not make use of some of the potential of this technology can any longer be justified from an educational viewpoint.

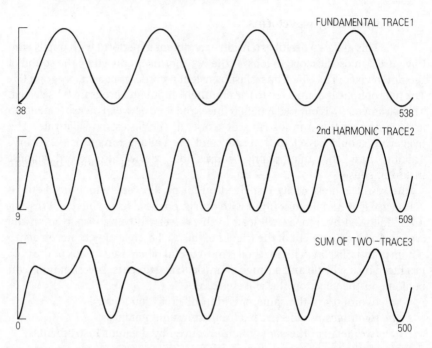

10.7 Sample waveform obtained with VELA

Notes and references

1 Claxton G. (1984) *Live and Learn: An Introduction to the Psychology of Growth and Change in Everyday Life.* Harper and Row, London.
2 These are made and sold by Instrumentation Software Ltd, 7 Gledhow Wood Avenue, Leeds LS8 1NY.
3 These are available from DATA (Scientific), 3 Windsor Rd, Linthorpe, Middlesbrough, Cleveland, TS5 6DS.
4 The MEP Analogue Sensor Manual available from Mrs Beth Bevis, Ronsella, Lordswood, Highbridge, Eastleigh, Hants SO5 7HR gives full details of sensors for those who wish to construct their own. For those who do not, there is a wide range marketed by Phillip Harris and Griffin & George.
5 A special cable for transferring data from the VELA is available from Educational Electronics, 28 Lake St, Leighton Buzzard, Beds. LU7 8RX, for connecting to common microcomputers.
6 Software for doing this on the BBC computer is available from Instrumentation Software Ltd, 7 Gledhow Wood Avenue, Leeds LS8 1NY.
7 The Mark 1 Vela does not have a + 5 V line on it and a 6 V battery is needed to supply this voltage.
8 Two other devices worth serious consideration are the *DataDisc* produced by Phillip Harris and the Unilab Interface made by Unilab. Both require a BBC computer for their use and the former is restricted in that it is not capable of recording more than a 100 readings a second which means that it will not record the waveforms from a microphone. For users of RML computers, a useful interface is marketed by ILECC, John Ruskin St, London SE5, which comes with accompanying software.
9 *Using the BBC Microcomputer in School Science Experiments.* (1986) The Association for Science Education, College Lane, Hatfield, Herts.

138

11 Physics and technology

1986 saw the introduction of the GCSE examination courses. Two of the aims in the National Criteria for physics[1] state that it should be taught

'To promote awareness and understanding of the social, economic, environmental and other implications of physics'. (Aim 2.2)

'To provide a basic basic knowledge and understanding of the principles and applications of physics which contribute to life in a technologically based society'. (Aim 2.3)

However, before embarking blindly down this path it is worth pausing to consider what is meant by the terms 'technology' and 'the contribution' of physics to 'life in a technologically based society. There is considerable confusion produced by the use of these terms for most people and at least a partial resolution is necessary if this aim is to be successfully pursued.

Pacey[2] highlights the confusion and distinguishes between the 'technical' aspect of technology, that is the knowledge, skills and techniques necessary for technological activity, and the cultural and organisational aspects of technology. The cultural aspect represents the goals, values and ethics associated with the practice of technology and the organisational aspect refers to the institutions such as factories, professional bodies and trades unions around whom much of this activity is based. Technological activity involves all three areas. Black & Harrison[3] have also used a broad definition of the nature of technology, seeing it as 'a disciplined process using resources of materials, energy and natural phenomena to achieve human purposes'.

Such a model sees science and physics as a restricted range of knowledge which makes a significant contribution to the practice of technology. However 'technology' draws on knowledge and value judgements from a whole range of areas as illustrated in figure 11.1. The knowledge provided by science and

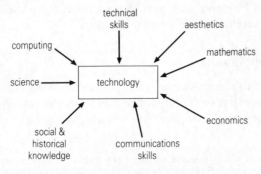

11.1 The practice of technology

139

physics is only one part of a much broader concept. The ASE[4] has undoubtedly recognised this and identified two strands of 'technology'.

(*a*) Technological activity which requires the student to 'design and make'.

(*b*) Technological awareness and appreciation.

The former is identified with Craft, Design and Technology and the latter with science. To develop 'technological awareness', the ASE see it as being necessary for science teachers to include some or all of the following activities in their lessons.

(*a*) Applying science to new situations in which there is a real need or problem thus involving the pupil in selecting appropriate scientific knowledge.

(*b*) Developing skills in designing and planning.

(*c*) Making judgements about the value of science in contexts other than laboratory science.

Science and technology are interrelated. The sort of science we investigate is often dependent on the technological problems to be solved. For example space travel represents a series of technological problems which have had a significant effect on the research directions of pure science. In the same way, Newton's laws of motion arose from the need to predict where cannon balls would go and the study of ballistics. Early steam engines were built with no firm understanding of the physical processes governing their operation; the study of thermodynamics arose because of the need to make steam engines more powerful and efficient.

What are the implications of this for the physics teacher? Science per se does not require technical applications to justify it as a human activity. Science seeks to expand the boundaries of human knowledge and understanding and no physics teacher is able to justify a syllabus simply in terms of its relevance. The knowledge of today may be the folklore of tomorrow. The essential difference between the current interpretation of 'technological relevance' and earlier ideas is that the current interpretation is to take the broad view of technology as defined by Black & Harrison. However there is much confusion abroad in the minds of both physics teachers and examiners and only the examinations will show which view has been taken. In its most restricted form, it would imply that many more questions in GCSE exams will be about the technical applications of physics. However, it is possible to identify three methods of approach to the links between physics and technology.

Technical applications

It is important to recognise that good physics teaching has always used technical examples of the applications of physics to provide relevance and meaning to the concepts it is developing. The following is a good example of such teaching.

> 'A first year lesson was introduced using an electric iron. The iron was taken apart to show the element and the sole plate. The construction of the plate was discussed with particular attention given to the thermostat and the way this controlled the temperature. A careful explanation was given showing a sense

140

of humour attractive to the pupils. The action of the thermostat was demonstrated and the hypothesis proposed that it was controlled by a Gremlin who switched the iron on or off whenever he got too hot or too cold. The pupils were obviously not able to accept such a hypothesis. Another iron was taken apart to show how the various controls were linked to the inside mechanism. As each part was removed the pupils were asked its purpose. Through careful control of the pupils' contributions the teacher led them to suggest how the automatic switching action controlled the temperature of the iron. Ultimately the idea of a bi-metallic strip was introduced and the pupils shown the two sides of metal. The effect of heat on the bi-metallic strip was demonstrated and pupils asked to note whether the metal always bent the same way. They were then asked to look for pattern in their observations and to provide explanations by questions such as, 'Why do you think it bends?', 'Which way will it bend?' 'What will happen if it cools?' and 'What will happen if I put it in a fridge?'. A number of bi-metallic strips were used to demonstrate the action of a fire alarm and the idea that the thermostat must be the reverse was introduced: in other words it switches off when it gets too hot. The teacher pointed out to the pupils that they still did not know why it bends. As lack of time prevented him from carrying out an experiment to find out, he introduced the running track analogy as a clue. Through structured discussion the pupils explained the mechanism. Finally blackboard diagrams were revealed showing the action of a bi-metallic strip in diagrams of the fairy light flasher, the thermostat in an electric iron and aquarium thermostat. An automatic choke from a car was demonstrated along with a coiled bi-metallic thermometer.'[5]

Applications that are relevant to the existing knowledge of the children are carefully interlaced with the teaching to provide relevance and meaning to the topic. Good physics teaching relies on such examples wherever suitable.

The great success of science has been in the technical application of the knowledge discovered. The action of a laser was theoretically predicted by Einstein in 1917 but not discovered till 1960. Who could have possibly predicted the many applications of this scientific discovery from compact discs to laser surgery? A text that shows many excellent applications of the principles of physics is *The World of Physics*[6] and the *Physics in Action* series[7]. However there is a wealth of material produced by independent and commercial organisations which are an invaluable resource to the physics teacher. The following is a summary of some of the main sources.

(a)   *Physics Plus*[8] is a set of materials produced by the Standing Conference on School Science and Technology. As well as a book containing many practical suggestions and illustrations of the application of physics, it is supplemented by many attractive and informative posters.

(b) The Electricity Council, British Telecom, British Gas, British Petroleum, the United Kingdom Atomic Energy Authority (UKAEA), the Centre for Alternative Technology: these organisations produce a large selection of materials ranging from poster to computer software at very modest prices for use in schools. A substantial amount of the material provides a useful illustration of the applications of physics within modern industry.

(c) The Institute of Physics provides a scheme for schools to affiliate to the Institute for a relatively small annual fee. For this they are provided with regular information on the materials produced by the Institute for schools and the magazines *Physics Education* and *Snippets*. The latter magazine provides many informative illustrations of the applications of physics. The Institute also produces a journal called *Physics and Technology* that gives a fuller treatment of some of the applications of physics. In addition, the Institute has a library of videos which schools can borrow which show many applications of physics.

(d) *Tomorrow's World*: television programmes like this are watched by many children and often provide useful illustrations of the applications of physics. They can act as a valuable stimulus to demonstrate some of the utility of a knowledge of physics in modern society.

(e) Visits: many organisations are often prepared to take parties of school children to show the work they do. Properly briefed in advance, these visits can be used as a focus for the application of physics in industry. Medical physics departments in hospitals are also often prepared to take parties of children. Such a visit is probably best suited to those that have done some radioactivity, but it often makes a fascinating visit which children can personally relate to. If physics does make such a significant contribution to modern technology, it should not be difficult to find a local application of it.

Physics in society

This perspective on physics is the one that aims to develop 'technological awareness' in the broad sense. There is little doubt that it causes teachers concern as such an approach inevitably takes them outside the bounds of their own narrow specialism. However, approached with enthusiasm, making use of the substantial wealth of resources available, there is no need for this to pose a threat to the teacher. The use and application of physics raises issues that may involve knowledge and skills from a wide range of areas, but the average teacher is substantially more knowledgeable than their pupils.

The other significant advantage of such an approach is that it is often this aspect of 'physics with a human face' that appeals to girls in providing meaning and relevance for much of the subject. Such an approach was taken successfully by the SCISP[9] course. It is true to say that many physics courses have primarily been written by men for boys and part of the explanation of the lack of appeal for girls must lie in this. Examples of the use of physics that consist of rockets and bullets cannot be described as appealing for the average girl. However the concept of physics as a subject which is actively involved in meeting human needs to provide a caring and better society is an aspect which appeals to what some writers have called 'feminine values'[10]. Many of the new materials, such as SATIS, emphasise this aspect and should be used to broaden the perspective of physics as a narrow, dry discipline. John Head[11] points to this when he says of pupils that 'science rarely seems to address their concern for personal identity and ideals'. Much of the material available emphasises the use of group discussion and presentation of work. Such a situation is unfamiliar to many physics teachers and demands a different role. However, this is necessary if pupils are to be allowed an opportunity to formulate value judgements about science and if science is to seem less authoritarian. The physics teacher will need to develop some of the skills of the history or social studies teacher.

There are three principal sources of materials that will probably be most useful to the science teacher.

Science and Technology in Society (SATIS)[12]

This is an excellent set of resource materials that covers the whole range of traditional science courses. It consists of seven books which focus on the use of science in society and the issues it raises. Each unit consists of teachers' notes and copyright-free worksheets. The exercises provided involve role plays, discussions, working in small groups to encourage cooperative activity, problem-solving activities and reading activities. The pack of materials was developed by the ASE to be used with existing science GCSE courses to provide a teaching resource to meet the needs of teachers confronted with reorganising their syllabuses in the light of the new GCSE criteria. The materials reflect a novel and imaginative approach to many of the issues and inevitably extend the science into other areas of the curriculum. The teachers' guide points to this when it says 'it has been found that non-science departments such as geography and personal and social education often show considerable interest'. The problem that can arise with these materials is that examination conscious pupils tend to see it as being peripheral to the examination. Such thinking reflects a very utilitarian view of school and education and needs to be challenged to inspire pupils into some awareness that the application of knowledge has a social dimension and implication.

The approach taken by SATIS is to insert relevant applications and issues at appropriate points in the science curriculum. Such an approach puts the science first. A more radical approach is to put the applications first and teach through applications. Such an approach has been taken in chemistry by *Salters Chemistry*[13], a GCSE course that approaches chemistry through issues. As yet no equivalent course exists in physics. Such an approach would be to start with an issue like nuclear power and to use this to focus on the need for energy in society and the methods of producing it and transferring it. This can lead to a more detailed consideration of electricity, its generation and the household electrics, covering the same fundamental physics but in reverse order. The approach in SATIS has been to take the former method, putting the science first, rather than the latter. There is a lot to be said for the latter approach, particularly with less able pupils, however most schools still tend to adopt the 'science first' approach slipping the applications in at suitable points. As confidence develops with the material, it is valuable to try alternative approaches.

Science in Society[14]

This course was produced by the ASE as a project and directed by John Lewis to try and meet some of the criticisms of narrowness of existing science courses. It consists of nine units and a teachers' guide and was principally aimed at lower sixth-formers with an examination at the end. It makes extensive use of simulation exercises and discussions, and although it has been criticised for the position it takes on some issues, it is a large resource of material. The unit of particular relevance to the teaching of physics is the unit on energy.

Science in a Social Context (SISCON)[15]

This is a similar course in that it aims to introduce children to the social aspects of science and was associated with an alternative O-level examination. It consists of eight readers which were designed to be used as a focus for discussion and project work. As such, much of the written material is probably too sophisticated for younger children, but it provides a valuable resource for teachers looking for materials to develop lessons on the social applications of science. The units that are probably particularly valuable to the teacher of physics are those on the Atomic Bomb; Energy: the Power to Work; Technology, Invention and Industry; Space, Cosmology and Fiction.

The other main area in physics where the application of physics in a social context has an obvious position is in the teaching of energy. As a topic, there are personal implications here in the use of energy in the home and a novel and interesting approach to this is taken by Nuffield Home Economics[16]. To some, it may seem strange to have a home economics book recommended in such a book as this. However, it concentrates on the use of energy in the home and, by focussing on the pupil's experience of this, it provides an approach that is substantially more meaningful for the less motivated pupil. Children are asked to study sources of energy, how it is transported and how it is 'used'. 'Saving Energy' is used as a means of introducing traditional concepts of conduction, convection and radiation. In addition, there is the potential here for many fascinating open-ended investigations. Does putting aluminium foil behind the radiator help to keep the room warmer? What type of draught-proofing material is the most effective? How much difference does cheap double-glazing make? The Department of Industry have produced a pack, *Energy in the Home*[17], which makes use of an excellent digital thermometer/light meter marketed by British Gas which provides the opportunity for many excellent investigations to be carried out. British Gas also markets a computer program called CEDRIC II which allows pupils to investigate the typical energy requirements of homes in the UK and the effect of insulation, double-glazing etc. Such activities, based in the 'real world' of pupils rather than the school science laboratory, act as a stimulus to pupils generating the desire for further knowledge.

Other useful materials are the videos/films *Time for Energy*[18] and *Energy in Perspective*[19]; both of these discuss the social issues in a stimulating and entertaining manner. *The Power Game*[20] is a computer program that places pupils in the position of supplying electrical energy on a national scale and in doing so raises technical issues about the physics of the transmission of electrical energy. Teachers looking for a more global perspective on the use of energy should look at the material from the Revised Nuffield Advanced Physics Course[21], Unit G. This contains a coherent and intelligent approach to the issues. In addition, British Petroleum publish a computer disc[22] with the global statistics for the use of energy which they will update annually. This can be used as the basis for investigations on the use of energy by a selected range of nations, a comparison of energy use in the western developed world, or the use of different energy sources throughout the world. The disc contains a substantial amount of data which could form the basis of much project work.

Physics as a 'problem-solving' activity

The basic process of technology is in many ways similar to the activity of the scientist as a problem solver. Woolnough & Allsop[23] have argued that the mnemonic PRIME should be used to help pupils identify the stages of problem solving in science. These stand for

- P for **Problems** to be tackled;
- R for **Research** into the appropriate factors;
- I for **Ideas** about the ways of tackling the problem;
- M for **Making** the device or the experiment;
- E for **Evaluating** the outcome;

The model used in technology can be summarised as

identification of problem;
design of a solution;
construction of solution;
evaluation of result.

Though the skills and knowledge required are often different, both activities are open-ended, requiring divergent, independent thinking by the student. Providing the opportunity for such activities in the classroom allows students to familiarise themselves with the approach used by real scientists and develop a tacit understanding of the nature of the technological process.

What kind of investigations are well suited to this approach? Physics teachers are only beginning to develop a repertoire of suitable investigations but the following list provides ideas for ones that have proved successful in the past.

- What makes a good parachute?
- What is the strongest and most attractive bridge that can be built from a limited supply of balsa wood to span 0.5 m?
- Make a vehicle driven by an elastic band that will go 1 m in the shortest time.
- Make a device to catch an egg falling from a height of 2 m without breaking.
- How can you keep a cup of tea hot for 30 minutes?
- How long does a standard battery last? Are Duracell batteries really worth paying the extra for?
- How efficient is a model electric motor? How can the efficiency be improved?
- What is the best gear on a bicycle for climbing a hill, low or high?
- How do you operate a nuclear power station to extract the maximum power from it?[24]
- What is the acceleration of a 100 m sprinter in the first metre?
- Design, using only a newspaper, an object which will support your weight a few centimetres off the ground.

This list merely provides a representative sample of ideas which can be used by teachers. A more extensive list can be obtained from BP Education service[25].

Pupils will need to be carefully briefed about the nature of the problem and given guidance with the resources and suitable techniques. An important comment by the HMI that is worth noting here is 'The best work was observed where the pupils had been carefully prepared for tackling technological problems; the underlying science was understood; and the pupils had access to the necessary resources.'[5]

Such investigations give children an opportunity to work creatively, originally and independently or in small groups, and the quality of the work can often be surprising even to the most jaundiced teacher. Pupils are encouraged to use their own communication skills. More importantly, the involvement of the pupil in the problem provides an opportunity to transcend the ritual of many standard physics lessons and the knowledge gained often becomes 'personalised' and meaningful. Most of all, this approach is the essence of the technological process.

Notes and references

1 *GCSE national criteria for Physics* (1986) HMSO, London.
2 Pacey A. (1983) *The Culture of Technology*. Blackwell, London.
3 Black P.J. & Harrison G. B. (1985) *In Place of Confusion–Technology and Science in the School Curriculum*. Loughborough, National College for Science & Technology.
4 Science & Technology. (1986) *Education in Science*, **120**, 27–8. The Science and Technology Sub-committee, Association for Science Education.
5 *Technology and School Science: an HMI Enquiry* (1985) HMSO, London.
6 Avison J. (1985) *The World of Physics*. Nelson.
7 Raitt G. (1987) *Physics in Action*. This is a series of six titles called *Heat and Temperature, Forces: Building a Cantilever Bridge, Electricity 1: Circuits, Electricity 2: Electromagnetism, Heat and Temperature*, and *Vibrations and Radiation*. They contain many modern, relevant applications of physics.
8 *Physics Plus* (1985) Hobsons/SCSST, Cambridge & London.
9 Schools Council Integrated Science Project (1972) Longmans.
10 Bentley D. & Watts D.M. (1986) 'Courting the positive virtues: a case for feminist science'. *European Journal of Science Education*, **8**, 2, 121–132.
11 Head J. (1985) *The Personal Response to Science*. Cambridge University Press.
12 *Science and Technology in Society (SATIS)*. Association for Science Education, College Lane Hatfield, Herts.
13 *Salters Chemistry* (1987) Science Education Group. Department of Chemistry, University of York.
14 Lewis J. (Prog. Director) (1981) *Science in Society*. Heinemann Educational Books.
15 Solomon J. (1983) *Science in a Social Context*. Blackwells.
16 *Nuffield Home Economics: People and Homes*. Teachers' Guide and Pupils' book (1985) Nuffield Chelsea Curriculum Trust.
17 *Energy in the Home*. Department of Trade and Industry.
18 *Time for Energy*. Shell Film Library, 25 The Burroughs, Hendon, London NW4 4AT.
19 *Energy in Perspective*. BP Film Library, 15 Beaconsfield Rd, London NW10 2LE.
20 *The Power Game: Understanding Electricity*. The Electricity Council.
21 Revised Nuffield Advanced Physics Course, Teachers' Guide and Students' Book (1986) Longmans. Unit G provides many relevant figures for the global use of energy.

22 *The Energy File*. BP Educational Service, Britannic House, Moor Lane, London EC2Y 9BU.
23 Woolnough B. & Allsop T. (1985) *Practical Work in Science*. Cambridge University Press.
24 This will need the computer program *Nuclear Reactor* published by Longmans.
25 *Investigation with Science*, BP Educational Service, Britannic House, Moor Lane, London EC2Y 9BU.

12 Computer-assisted learning in physics

The introduction of the cheap microcomputer and a wide range of software has had a significant impact on the potential learning experiences for children. Too often commentators on CAL (Computer Assisted Learning) tend to concentrate on aspects of the software. However as Ellis[1] has observed 'thinking about the computer's role in education does not mean thinking about computers, it means thinking about education'. The key criterion in such evaluation is the *nature of the learning experiences offered*. Programs and software have to be evaluated as educational materials and an evaluative framework is necessary if objective statements are to supplant mere subjective impressions. Kemmis[2] suggested classifying programs by the possible learning experiences they can provide and proposed that types of software could be classified by four categories; instructional, revelatory, conjectural and emancipatory. Though many items of software often combine two of these categories, this is still one of the most useful frameworks for making a judgement of the educational value of such materials and their suitability for the preferred teaching style of the individual teacher. These can be applied usefully to most physics software which falls into the following categories.

Demonstration programs

This class of programs is often referred to under the generic term of 'electronic blackboard' programs and falls into the category of instructional programs. Here the computer is used by the teacher as a sophisticated visual aid and the graphical and animation features are often paramount. Two good examples of this type of software are *Transverse Waves II*[3] and *Young's Slits*[4].

In *Transverse Waves II* an animated transverse wave is displayed on the screen whose frequency, amplitude and velocity can be adjusted by the teacher. The specifically transverse nature of the wave can be shown by highlighting one particle in the wave. A second wave and the sum of the first and the second can be displayed (figure 12.1). The teacher can adjust the phase relationship of the first two waves so that the package can be used to vividly display the concepts of 'constructive' and 'destructive' interference. In addition the phenomenon of 'beats' can be shown by adjusting the frequency of the second wave so that it differs from the first by a small amount. There is no other form of animated visual display that provides the teacher with such a powerful expression of such ideas. Additionally, this software provides the opportunity to answer children's conjectural questions of the form 'What happens if the second wave has twice the amplitude of the first?'

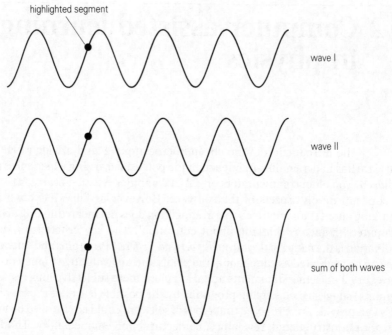

highlighted segment

wave I

wave II

sum of both waves

12.1 Screen display for *Transverse Waves II*

Young's Slits shows how the waves from two sources in phase superpose to produce an interference pattern. Two animated waves from separate sources are produced on the display and converge on a point on the screen. The teacher can move the point of convergence up and down the screen, gradually constructing the resultant amplitude which is shown on the right of the screen

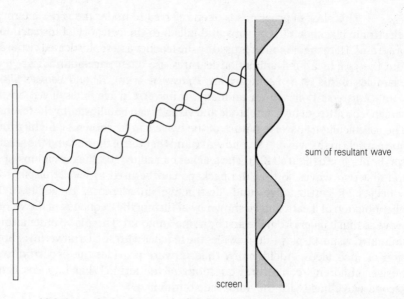

sum of resultant wave

screen

12.2 Screen display for *Young's Slits*

150

(figure 12.2). It is possible to vary the wavelength, the separation of the sources and the frequency of the waves so that the effect on the final pattern produced can be fully explored.

The facilities to explore a physical reality are much better than those available in the nearest substitute, the plastic waves pinned to the side of the board. Such packages can be used as revelatory packages where the child can explore the phenomena, if the computer and the CAL software are used as one station in a circus of experiments. In the above example, pupils can be given sets of exercises requiring them to answer questions like these.

(a) What are the conditions for constructive interference?
(b) How is the interference pattern broadened so that the maxima are further apart?
(c) By taking measurements from the screen, what relationship exists between the maxima separation and the source separation?

One class of programs that fall into this category which should be avoided are programs which purport to instruct pupils about pressure or electrical circuits. No CAL software has a teacher's capability to assess the needs of an individual learner and respond critically with an appropriate explanation. Such software has a fixed model of the students and provides limited explanations that could often more appropriately be provided by text or video. The only effective, but limited, potential of such instructional programs is that their drill and practice routines provide an opportunity to reinforce skills and knowledge learnt previously elsewhere.

Simulations

Simulations of real events in physics model a process in reality. These programs allow the learner the opportunity to alter the parameters of the system and examine what happens. This exposure to a working model of a physical system is said by Kemmis *et al.* to be a revelatory learning experience. The learner can test out what will happen, and this is often done by printing out a table of results or a graph. They can then compare this with their knowledge and model of the phenomenon. This comparison and evaluaton provides an opportunity to construct an understanding of the behaviour of the system, partially by trial and error and partially by logic.

One of the best examples of this type of program is the *Nuclear Reactor Simulation*[5]. This simulates the component parts of the complete advanced gas-cooled nuclear reactor: the core, the carbon dioxide heat exchanger and the turbine system. Pupils can investigate the behaviour of each component separately and then finish by trying to run the whole system at maximum efficiency. To do this requires a full understanding of the various sections of the reactor and this is best done by asking the students to work as a group on the task. Watson[6] has pointed to the fact that in such group collaboration 'they may also be learning how to communicate ideas among themselves, to formu- late arguments and logical paths of thought through the demands of group decision making'. The teacher's role in such an activity is that of a resource, intervening at the critical moments to provide the knowledge necessary to make a better decision and guiding the group through a sensible route of activities. This particular simulation shows another advantage of such materials which is that they provide the pupil with experience of a working physical reality, albeit a model, that is not possible by other methods. Simulations are commonly used for phenomena that are too dangerous, too fast or too slow to observe, or too difficult to perform in the laboratory.

Another simulation that shows many of these features is *Power Package*[7]. This simulates the operation of a small section of the National Grid for the supply of electricity. The group is placed in the position of supply manager and have to decide which stations to run at various times during the day, when to overhaul, how to respond to peak demands and provide an economic but reliable supply. Obviously such a package does not restrict the knowledge required to simply physics as some of the decisions require social and economic knowledge. However, it is a useful role play activity which simultaneously illustrates an application of physics and generates a better understanding of the electricity supply network.

Such programs were not designed to be used as instructional programs and attempts to do so by teachers are unlikely to be effective. As the students investigate the system, they may come to a better understanding of the model which is gradually revealed to them through its behaviour under different parameters. The program also allows learners to conjecture and hypothesise. However, the main class of programs that do this are models and microworlds.

Models and microworlds

Modelling is an important activity for physicists who construct symbolic, analytical models of the observed physical reality and test them against experimental results. As better theories are derived, the models can be refined to achieve a closer correspondence with reality and, through this process, a better understanding can be reached. All the simulations referred to previously contain mathematical models of how the system behaves where the student can alter the initial parameters and observe the effect. Modelling for secondary school pupils would allow pupils to construct their own models and observe their behaviour. The computer language LOGO provides a powerful model in which some simple models can be constructed. A model for the random walk was shown in chapter 6 on waves. The following is one for circular motion which could possibly be produced by issuing the challenge 'Write a program which will make the turtle go in a circle'.

```
Program to make the turtle go in a circle:
            TO CIRCLE
            REPEAT 360 [FD 1 RT 1]
            END
```

Although brief, it illustrates one important physical principle, that to go in a circle the object must turn in towards the centre and that to do this a force will be required in this direction. More elaborate models can be constructed by those pupils who are more familiar with this programming language.

The *Dynamic Modelling System (DMS)*[8] is probably the best known environment available for modelling. The user can set up any sort of linear model and investigate its behaviour using tabular or graphical output. The models used are said to be 'iterative'. Essentially what this means is that the system takes the initial values, calculates a set of new values according to the model inserted and then uses these values to calculate how it will behave in the next step. A simple model of free fall using this is shown below.

A = acceleration
V = velocity   DV = change in velocity
S = displacement   DS = change in displacement
T = time   DT = time interval

Physics of the model	Representation in DMS
Increase in velocity = acceleration × time interval	$DV = A*DT$
New velocity = old velocity + change in velocity	$V = V + DV$
Increase in displacement = velocity × time interval	$DS = V*DT$
New displacement = old displacement + change in S	$S = S + DS$
New time = old time + time interval	$T = T + DT$

Such a model has to be provided with a set of initial values which may be:

Time	= 0	$T = 0$
Time interval	= 0.1	$DT = 0.1$
Acceleration	= 10	$A = 10$
Displacement	= 0	$S = 0$
Velocity	= 0	$V = 0$

The modelling system can then be made to run the model and to produce a graph of distance or velocity against time. The behaviour can then be compared with reality and parameters of the model easily edited to include the effects of air friction if necessary. Since the force of air friction is proportional to the square of velocity and in the opposite direction to the motion, this is done by adding the following line to the model.

$$A = 10 - C*V*V \quad \text{and giving a value to } C = 0.01$$

The difference between modelling on a microcomputer and simulations is that modelling allows the student to adjust the model rather than interact with a predetermined model. The purpose is to provide insight and not numbers. Again such activities are best done collaboratively with worksheets and documentation provided by the teacher as part of a circus of activities. As yet, few teachers of physics have developed substantial experience of modelling within secondary schools, but with new powerful visual modelling tools, such as STELLA[9], the is little doubt that it will play a greater role in coming years.

Microworlds can best be described as a halfway house between modelling and simulations. Flexible models of reality are simulated on the microcomputer that allow the user a substantial degree of freedom to investigate the behaviour of the system. The most well known are dynamics microworlds that model Newtonian environments, allowing the pupil to play and manoeuvre the object presented on the screen. *Mobile* and *Newtonian games*[10] are examples of this. Typically the user can apply thrust to the object with a 'rocket' in one of four directions. The walls of the screen are perfectly elastic and the force of friction and gravity, initially set to zero can be changed over a range of values. Additionally the mass of the object can be varied. The pupil is encouraged to explore and tackle certain predefined tasks, such as stopping the rocket or making it move in a circle. The intention is to provide an opportunity for some experiential learning through which the pupil would develop an intuitive understanding of Newtonian dynamics. Since current approaches to teaching this topic notably fail to provide such opportunities, this represents one means of achieving this.

Emancipatory packages

Although pupils now make extensive use of calculators to free them from some of the effort of arithmetical manipulation, teachers have so far failed to make use of some of the potential software on the microcomputer. These allow pupils to overcome their limited skills and develop their confidence in physics. *Patterns*[11] is a package which allows pupils to enter experimental results and perform calculations on the data and present them in an attractive graphical manner. The results can be printed out for a permanent record in the pupils' book. Pupils should be encouraged to manually produce such graphs, but such tools can help in inspiring confidence and developing a sense of achievement which is often not provided by other methods.

Also in this category is the substantial number of CAL packages which allow the microcomputer to be interfaced to experiments. They can be a powerful tool which allow the user to collect data accurately, repetitively and efficiently. The software will then display the data in a graphical or tabular form, perform statistical operations and produce a permanent printed copy of the results. This provides the pupil with a modern powerful tool of the experimental scientist. Again, pupils need to develop the manual skills of observation and data collection, but such apparatus is particularly powerful for observing many transient events which cannot be recorded by hand such as voltage traces from a microphone and the change in current through a bulb as it is turned on.

It is important to note that none of these categories imply the substitution of the machine and its software for the teacher. Teachers have the advantage of being responsive and flexible to the infinite variety of individual needs they meet in the classroom which no computer program can ever do. What the CAL software is capable of providing is an alternative learning experience for the child which may be effective in achieving a level of understanding that more traditional means are currently failing to reach.

Notes and references

1 Ellis A. (1974) *The Use and Misuse of Computers*. McGraw Hill, New York.
2 Kemmis S. (1977) *How do Students Learn? Working Papers on Computer Assisted Learning*. Centre for Applied Research in Education, Occasional Publications No 5 University of East Anglia.
3 *Transverse Waves II*. Heinemann, London.
4 *Young's Slits*. Heinemann, London.

5 *The Nuclear Reactor Simulation* (1985) Longmans. This was developed by the *Computers in the Curriculum* project in conjunction with the UKAEA, and the model used is supposedly very realistic.

6 Watson D.W. in Kelly A.V. (1985) *Microcomputers in the Curriculum.* Harper & Row.

7 *Power Package. Understanding Electricity.* The Electricity Council.

8 *The Dynamic Modelling System* (1986) Longmans. Alghough primarily intended for use in A-level physics, the system does have potential for use in elementary dynamics. Models have also been published for use in chemistry, economics, biology and geography. Further details can be found in Ogborn J. & Wong D. (1984) 'A microcomputer Dynamic Modelling System', *Physics Education,* **19**, 138–142.

9 STELLA is a graphical modelling system available from LOGOTRON in the UK for the Macintosh computer.

10 *Mobile.* Science in Process Software, Capital Media, ILECC, John Ruskin St, London SE5, and *Newtonian Games* (1986) Macmillan.

11 *Patterns.* Science in Process Software, Capital Media, John Ruskin St, London SE5.

13 Girls and physics

It is a matter of considerable concern that girls, when offered a free choice, opt away from physical science in large numbers. The concern is both for society as a whole, which is under-utilising a scarce resource, and for individuals who may be denied opportunities of employment in scientific and technical careers. The exact nature of the problem is shown in figure 13.1[1].

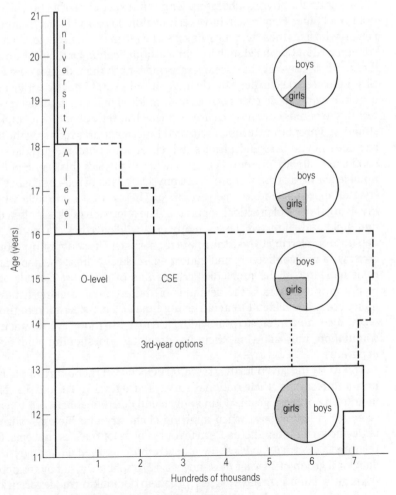

13.1 The Physics Teaching Pyramid for 1983–4

157

Many aspects have been identified as contributory factors to the problem. Physics is often approached through a conceptual framework that lacks relevant applications and gives the appearance that the subject lacks any connection with the real world; physics makes extensive use of a mathematical formalism to articulate many of its important ideas. However the problem is often not the mathematics itself, as mathematics does not suffer from a lack of girls willing to study the subject to a high level. One author[2] has suggested that the problem is the reductionism used in physics. The process of tackling a problem by removing clearly relevant features, such as ignoring air friction in the dynamics of a falling ball, seems arbitrary and is a game that they find difficult to accept. The subject rarely touches the affective domain to which girls give a higher priority. There seems to be little room for expression of feelings or emotions in the subject and most physics laboratories help to contribute towards these images, often presenting a cold, dull environment with cupboards crammed with outmoded technical gadgets.

Girls enter the physics laboratory with little experience of technical activities from the home. They rarely have technical hobbies and father/brother is the person who fixes those technical objects that fail in the household. They are not convinced that they need such a technical qualification for their future employment, which anyway may seem less significant to them than it does for boys. Girls who are asked to describe their life situation at 30 have clear ideas which are often expressed in terms of husband, children and specific dwelling characteristics, whereas boys have clearly formed ideas only about their employment situation. Parents and teachers will readily accept a girl expressing the fact that she does not understand physics, which acts to reinforce any lack of self-confidence already present. For the teacher of physics this is one of the most notable features of girls' approach to physics, a lack of self-confidence in their style of approach and less perseverance. This is most noticeable with work involving the use of practical apparatus. The approach of girls is often diffident and timid and, in mixed classes, many girls will leave boys to manipulate the apparatus preferring to take the role of rapporteur. The contrasting approach of boys, who will confidently and almost aggressively abuse the apparatus, is a clear indicator of the problem. Perhaps one of the most difficult problems confronting teachers is the demands of the attention-seeking behaviour of many boys. It is difficult to avoid giving time and consideration to those who seem keen and interested, providing them with more eye contact, verbal stimulation and allowing them to dominate questioning and access to apparatus.

The APU[3] has given further research evidence of the nature of the problem from the results of their national surveys at ages 11, 13 and 15. National monitoring of these groups found only small differences between the average score for girls and boys when applying chemistry and biology concepts but large and systematic differences in favour of boys for physics concepts. In items relating to electricity, boys show an even more marked advantage. The APU data for a group of 11 year olds shows a 42/6 split (42% of boys as opposed to 6% of girls claiming to have played with them) for making models from kits, 59/30 for playing snooker or similar games, 45/16 split for playing with toy electricity sets and 50/23 for making models with Lego. Similar patterns are demonstrated for using measuring instruments, watching television pro-grammes and general interest in scientific applications. The overriding mes-sage of this is that girls bring to the physics classroom a substantially poorer set of prior experiences of making things, taking them apart again and generally tinkering.

The solution demands an approach which is multi-faceted and reflects the nature of the problem. It would be foolish to pretend that the physics teacher can compensate for the nature of society; however, they can make efforts to redress the problem. One of the most significant interventions is the influence of the HMI document *Science 5–16: A Statement of Policy*[4]. The policy that all pupils should experience a 'broad and balanced' science curriculum means that fewer schools will be offering children the choice to do only one science. This should result in more girls doing physics and more boys doing biology. Increasingly physics will be taught as part of a coordinated, modular or integrated science syllabus which will mean that more girls will have an extended education in the physical sciences. *However, this by itself will not solve the problem* of girls' experience of physics which, if taught in the same manner, will remain uninterested and antipathetic, resulting in no increase in numbers opting to study the subject at A-level or pursue a technical career in further education. Teachers of physics must recognise that physics is never used in society without value judgements being made as to the potential benefits and disadvantages. Girls, and boys, must be encouraged and given an opportunity to express views which many physics teachers may consider emotional and unscientific because they involve realms of knowledge that are not physics. Only if this can happen can girls begin to recognise that the work of a physicist is a human activity that has important consequences for humanity. Ultimately physics must have a human face which implies a challenge to the physics teacher to incorporate the applications of physics in society as a basic feature in their teaching rather than something to be quietly slipped in at the end of a topic. Part of the success of the SCISP[5] course in appealing to girls was the manner in which it integrated applications and content. The teacher of physics needs to look harder at the approaches of such courses and materials such as SATIS[6] to extract relevant material.

Another approach adopted by some schools is to ensure that girls are taught physics separately. Such an environment prevents the domination by confi-dent and extrovert boys, allowing the teacher to organise activities of discus-sion and group collaboration and providing an opportunity to voice their natural concerns and develop confidence with the material and apparatus. In this situation the girls can be actively involved in the learning strategy. Too many lessons in physics are presented as 'mystery tours' where the purpose and knowledge is revealed at the end. This sense of purposelessness does not help to build confidence and teachers should actively attempt to involve pupils in the lesson and develop a sense of trust. The advantage of this approach is that it allows the teacher to recognise that there is a difference in learning style between the sexes. The conceptual nature of physics and the conflict between the scientific and the life-world meanings means that knowledge often results from a period of conflict and crisis which results in accommodation and equilibration. This implies a readiness to take risks for which the students must be prepared carefully, making them aware of the feelings it is likely to generate and the need to persist. Many girls feel unhappy about advancing to new topics when the existing topic of study has not been completely mastered and, threatened with insecurity, resort to rules and formulae that do not provide a good understanding of the subject. An all-female environment may provide the teacher with a better atmosphere to deal with these insecurities and reinforce the confidence of girls. The objection to this approach is that since our society itself is a mixed society, to separate girls from boys is only a temporary solution, and that this merely delays the eventual problem. In addition it is possible for teachers to develop different attitudes and expectations which lead to the girls being offered an inferior science education. However, it is an important age, when crucial decisions are made that have implications for life. To provide an environment in which confidence and interest in the subject can develop should be seriously considered. It is the teacher's expectations which are possibly more important than anything else. It is essential to make it plainly obvious that

(a) physics is considered by the teacher to be a subject that is as important to girls as it is to boys;

(b) scientific careers for girls are just as viable as they are for boys and that there are many employers who will welcome a woman returning after a break in her career to have children;

(c) girls will be treated seriously in the class and that noisy and assertive boys will be prevented from dominating the attention and eye contact of the teacher. One way of achieving this is to ensure that the girls sit near the front where they will naturally attract more attention. This also prevents them from sliding into the recesses of the classroom.

What is also needed is a re-evaluation of the image of physics that is presented to children. Physics often appears as a cold, unemotional subject that is deterministic with no room for discussion or debate. The examples that are discussed, such as cars, rockets and levers, seem to have little relevance to the female perspective which is fundamentally more caring and human-centred. A sense of balance can be introduced with exemplars based in medicine, the home and the human body. The approach taken by Nuffield Home Economics[7] to the teaching of electricity, which in focussing on the home, makes the subject substantially more meaningful for boys as well as girls, is a good example. The human body is an excellent demonstration of the use of levers as distance-multipliers and the teaching of the transfer of energy by heat could be done by examining the question 'How do we keep our homes warm?' The habit of writing so many observations in the impersonal third person should be varied. Young children should be provided with an opportunity to write creatively or just jot down notes about their observations and thoughts. Try asking them to write a letter to their brother/sister explaining what they did and learnt in physics or a report for the school newsletter. This has the effect of changing the audience and allowing the personal into their thinking.

Textbooks need careful examination for their use of sexist terminology and illustrations that display men in active roles and, either lack illustrations of women or display them in traditional, passive roles. Physics courses are notoriously written by men for boys and taught by men. Textbook writers are beginning to correct this fault but they need to be examined carefully. Limited research evidence shows that the role model presented by the teacher is not as important as the quality of the teaching. What is required is teaching that is enthusiastic and varied, linking theory and practical to everyday examples, and which provides an opportunity for children to formulate and express their ideas.

Up-to-date careers information is produced by the Equal Opportunities Commission[8], including many posters of girls who have followed scientific careers and amusing posters of the consequence of not following such a career path. The Institute of Physics[9] has also devoted much attention to this and produces many posters and leaflets on career opportunities in physics specifically aimed at girls.

Perhaps the most important thing to remember though is that it is possible to get large numbers of girls to study physics in a mixed comprehensive environment. A study carried out in Hertfordshire on 'Attitudes to Science' found a number of schools with large numbers studying physics to 16 +. In one school 54% of the girls chose to study physics in the fourth year. The first step to finding a solution is to recognise the problem[10]. What are the numbers and percentages of girls studying physics in the fourth and fifth year in your school?

Finally the same sorts of issues that have been raised concerning equal opportunities for girls occur within the context of physics education in a multi-cultural society. There is, for instance, the danger that all science will be presented as being the product of a white Caucasian society. Examples of the use of physics can, and should, be drawn from other cultural backgrounds. It is easy to give the implicit assumption that high technology provides the best solutions. It is easy to forget that only one third of the world has mains electricity supplies in their homes. Solutions to the technological problem of how to keep milk cool are very culturally dependent. A refrigerator may be a good solution in the UK, but in Sudan there may well be no refrigerator available and then no means of supplying it with power. A better solution would be to use an evaporative cooler of unglazed pottery. This is a cheap and effective solution that can be made locally. This also raises the issues of the disparity of the provision of resources which should not be avoided just because this is physics.

The crux of the matter lies in teacher expectations. Does it matter if the pupil is called Denise, Dennis or Aqbal?

Notes and references

1 *Statistics on Physics Education* (1984) Institute of Physics.
2 Beyer K. & Reich J. (1987) *Why are girls inhibited from learning scientific concepts in physics?* Paper presented at the GASAT 4 conference.
3 *Girls and Physics. APU Occasional paper 4* (1986) Sandra Johnson & Patricia Murphy DES.
4 Science 5–16: A Statement of Policy (1985) HMI. HMSO, London.
5 Schools Council Integrated Science Project. (1972) Longmans.
6 *Science and Technology in Society.* (1986) Association for Science Education.

7 Nuffield Home Economics course is published for Nuffield Chelsea Curriculum Trust by Hutchinson Education (1982).
8 The Equal Opportunities Commission, Overseas House, Quay St, Manchester, M3 3HN.
9 The Institute of Physics, Schools Affiliation Service, 47 Belgrave Square, London SW1.
10 Two important documents that provide a substantial information on the nature of the problems and possible solutions are (*a*) *Girls and Physics: Reflections on APU survey findings*. Johnson S. & Murphy P. (1986) DES. and (*b*) *Better Science: For both girls and boys*. Curriculum Guide 6. (1987) Secondary Science Curriculum Review. Heinemann.

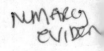

Mathematics in physics to GCSE

Most of the mathematics involved in physics courses to GCSE is relatively simple for the teacher, but not for the pupils! The research team of the Concepts in Secondary Mathematics and Science project concluded 'The results of the CSMS research have far-reaching implications for the teaching of mathematics at the secondary level. The overwhelming impression obtained is that mathematics is a *very difficult* subject for most children'[1]. The book from which this quotation is drawn is important reading for all teachers of science. It is very easy to underestimate the difficulties encountered by children. Teachers of physics must remember that they are inevitably teachers of mathematics because of the numerical nature of the subject and they are strongly advised to consult their colleagues in the mathematics department for advice and guidance.

The main difficulties arise with the concept of proportion which most children find very difficult prior to the age of 15. Basically this is because it is an abstract concept which Piagetians would say requires formal operational thinking. This means that it should be approached with great care and illustrated with statements to the effect that 'doubling the force, doubles the extension' for a spring, and 'doubling the force, doubles the acceleration' for an accelerating object. The CSMS research found that whereas only 15% of all fourth years could cope with questions that required a full understanding of proportion, 97% could cope with the simpler formulation.

The Science APU unit has also found that children have difficulties with problems that require representing quantities with continuous variables. So graphs of force against extension are drawn as bar charts rather than line graphs because they do not see that the measurements represent a selection of a continuous range of a variable. Unfortunately work with ticker tapes does not help to correct this. The CASE[2] project has produced materials designed to accelerate childrens' thinking with continuous variables and their relationships, and teachers may find these materials useful.

The main difficulty arises for children when they need to rearrange an equation to find an unknown quantity. Teachers should remember that many pupils find extreme difficulty with relationships expressed algebraically. It is better to express relationships in the form of words so that pupils can attach a physical meaning to them. Hence

$$\text{power} = \text{volts} \times \text{amps} \quad \text{is better than} \quad P = VI$$

and

$$\text{energy transferred} = \text{force} \times \text{distance} \quad \text{is better than} \quad E = Fd$$

163

The difficulties arise with problems that specify two quantities and require a third, such as 'What size fuse would you fit in the plug of a mains (240 V)-operated 300 W televison?' The simplest approach for pupils with numerical difficulties is to insert the numbers in the relevant equation

$$300 \text{ W} = 240 \text{ V} \times \text{amps}$$

The pupils can then be asked to use their calculators to find what the number of amps must be so that 240 times this number comes to 300. The obvious number to try is 1.5 which gives an answer that is too large. Further sophistication of trial-and-error methods will finally produce the right answer and this is the easiest method for children.

The approach that modern maths takes is to see the equation as a transformation. 'Volts' is a function which accepts 'amps' as an input and 'maps' this into power.

amps ⟶ │ × volts │ ⟶ power

Inverting the function reverses the direction of the procedure so that power becomes an input to the inverse function ' ÷ volts' which maps this into amps.

amps ⟵ │ ÷ volts │ ⟵ power

So to obtain the answer to the question, it is merely necessary to divide the power by the volts and the answer will be in amps. This may seem inordinately long-winded but the advantage is that the process is familiar to pupils from their work in mathematics, whereas the adult habit of cross-multiplying and rearranging the equation is not. The adult habit can be introduced as a useful short-cut as more problems of this kind are done.

Another standard approach to such equations with three unknowns is to write all the elements in a triangle. The most well-known of these is the Ohm's Law Triangle (figure A.1). The simple rule applied here is that to find the unknown quantity you cover it with your finger. An examination of the triangle then shows that

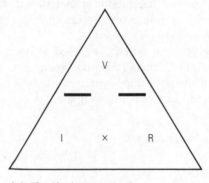

A.1 The Ohm's Law triangle

$$V = I \times R$$
$$I = V/R$$
$$R = V/I$$

Obviously such a method could be applied to other equations such as $F = ma$ or 'Energy transferred = force × distance'. This approach may be instrumental but helps to develop pupils' confidence.

Finally it is important to remember that mathematical equations as used in physics differ significantly from mathematical equations in that they represent physical quantities. This means that we should attempt to include these quantities in all equations, so that we would write

$$\text{energy transferred} = 5 \text{ N} \times 4 \text{ m}$$
$$= 20 \text{ J}$$

If introduced from the beginning of the course, it has the advantage of conditioning pupils to the use of units within equations which is an important aspect of the use of mathematics in physics. Most examination boards deduct marks for the omission of units.

References

1 Hart K.M. (gen. editor) (1981) *Children's Understanding of Mathematics: 11–16*. John Murray.
2 *Cognitive Acceleration through Science Experiments Project*. Centre for Educational Studies, Kings' College, 552 Kings Rd, London SW10 OUA.

Further reading

The following is a list of books that teachers would find useful sources and references in preparing materials for their lessons.

Revised Nuffield Physics: Teachers' Guides Years 3, 4 and 5. (1977) Longmans.

These books are the only books that cover the teaching of physics in substantial detail. As well as covering the content with many useful suggestions and approaches, they provided detailed illustrations and guides to the experiments. Many schools still have the original versions of the Nuffield materials which were issued as separate teachers' guides and 'Guides to the experiments'. Teachers need to remember that this course was aimed at the top quartile of the school population so that much of the approach is unsuitable for lower ability or mixed ability classes, but as a general guide to some of the ideas it is very useful. In addition, these books and their curriculum thinking are founded in ideas prevalent in the 1960s. Ideas of what are appropriate curriculum materials and approaches have changed substantially since, for example these books take no account of the lack of girls interested in physics and how the course might be altered to make the materials more attractive to them.

Avison J. (1984) *The World of Physics.* Nelson.

This is an excellent book for teachers looking for a clear, modern and relevant exposition of much of the physics in present GCSE courses. Although a pupil's textbook, much of it is too demanding in terms of its reading age. It also contains many excellent illustrations of the applications of physics.

Warren J. (1979) *Understanding Force.* John Murray.

Warren has been a long-standing critic of many of the failures of physics teachers to communicate and understand the basic physics concepts in force and mechanics. Teachers wishing to avoid similar traps will find this lucid account invaluable.

Driver R. (1983) *The Pupil as Scientist.* Open University Press.

This short book is an invaluable and cogent account of many of the difficulties experienced by pupils in coming to an understanding of the many concepts presented in science and particularly physics. Its clear exposition is essential reading for all teachers of science who wish to understand their own situation more effectively and act on it.

Osborne R. & Freyberg P. (1985) *Learning in Science.* Heinemann.

This book summarises in a clear and lucid form much of the work of the 'alternative conceptions' movement. Teachers will find it useful to read to check their own ideas and develop an awareness of some of the common misconceptions held by pupils about the nature of physical phenomena.

Rogers E. (1960) *Physics for The Enquiring Mind*. Princetown University Press.

Rogers has a natural gift for communicating some of the complex ideas of physics in a style that is readable and entertaining. Despite its voluminous size, this book would help teachers who found the more traditional accounts confusing or unhelpful.

Physical quantities and their units

The most important aspect of units that the teacher should understand is the representation of units such as those of velocity and pressure. Expressed in normal language we say an object has a velocity of '5 metres per second' or that there is a pressure of '10 000 newtons per metre squared'. The accepted scientific notation is 5 ms^{-1} for the velocity and $10\,000 \text{ N m}^{-2}$ for the pressure. However most pupils find this representation difficult and fail to see what it is expressing. For the examples given then, it is much better to write 5 m/s^2 and $10\,000 \text{ N/m}^2$. The same is true of all units that involve the use of the expression 'per'.

Physics teachers make use of one non-SI unit when they are teaching motion. This is the centimetre/ten-tick (cm/tt). The reason for this is that the centimetre is still a very convenient measure of small distances which are encountered in the teaching of motion with ticker tape. Similarly, the fact that the ticker timer physically puts dots on the tape at regular intervals in time makes it easy to quantify time in terms of the number of ticks on the tape. The unit of a ten-tick is a segment of time which generally produces distances travelled of the order of several centimetres which can be conveniently pasted in the average school textbook. That which we choose to teach and the way in which we teach is inevitably conditioned by the technology available.

In writing units and their symbols it is normal to use lower-case except when the unit is named after a person, in which case the *symbol* is written in capital letters, for example becquerel, Bq. All physical quantities are the product of a *numerical value* (pure number) and a *unit*. All units are based on seven independent physical quantities which are separately determined. These are shown in table A.1

Table A.1

Physical quantity	Base unit
length	metre
mass	kilogram
time	second
electric current	ampere
thermodynamic temperature	kelvin
amount of substance	mole
luminous intensity	candela

Table A.2 shows the main units used in the teaching of physics to age 16. The recommended format to be used is given. The representation in brackets is the representation agreed under the International System of Units (SI).

Table A.2

Quantity	Base unit for quantity	Symbol	Abbreviated unit	Equivalent unit
mass	kilogram	m	kg	
length	metre	l	m	
time	second	t	s	
force	newton	F	N	
velocity	metre/second	v	m/s (ms^{-1})	
acceleration	metre/ second squared	a	m/s² (ms^{-2})	
pressure	pascal	P	Pa	N/m²
density	kilogram/ cubic metre	ρ	kg/m³ (kg m^{-3})	
charge	coulomb	Q	C	
current	ampere	I	A	C/s
voltage	volt	V	V	J/C
resistance	ohm	R	Ω	
Celsius temperature	degrees Celsius	t	° C	
thermodynamic temperature	degrees Kelvin	T	K	
specific heat capacity		c	J/kg K ($\text{J kg}^{-1}\text{ K}^{-1}$)	
energy				
(i) thermal energy	joule	Q	J	
(ii) energy transferred	joule	W	J	
power	watt	P	W	J/s
wavelength	metre	λ	m	
frequency	hertz	f	Hz	
activity of a radioactive source	becquerel	A	Bq	

When abbreviated, units are always singular so '3 cm' is correct and '3 cms' would be wrong. In addition many physical units are given prefixes to indicate multiples and sub-multiples. The ones commonly used in teaching physics up to age 16 are shown in table A.3.

Table A.3

Multiple	Prefix	Symbol	Submultiple	Prefix	Symbol
10^3	kilo	k	10^{-2}	centi	c
10^6	mega	M	10^{-3}	milli	m
10^9	giga	G	10^{-6}	micro	μ
10^{12}	tera	T	10^{-9}	nano	n
			10^{-12}	pico	p

The ASE document *SI Units, Signs, Symbols and Abbreviations* (3rd edition, ASE, 1981) should be consulted by those seeking further information in this area.

Index